THIS IS THE DESERT

The Story of America's Arid Region

by PHIL AULT

Illustrated by LEONARD EVERETT FISHER

THE American desert covers approximately one-sixth of the United States. Although it knows few rivals in natural beauty, the endless miles of hot sands, lack of moisture and soaring temperatures have proved a formidable challenge to man's ingenuity. The desert's story is one of tragedy, humor and fabulous events.

Here is Death Valley, scene of disaster in the opening of the West as nature took its toll in thirst and starvation. Here are ghost towns and tales of prospectors rich overnight, recalling a fantastic era. Dinosaur tracks that hint of ancient lush forests, mysterious giant Indian figures, Death Valley Scotty's "castle," the U. S. Army Camel Corps, the engineering feat that created Hoover Dam, colorful 20-mule borax teams, Coronado's search for fabled cities of gold—all are part of the drama of the desert, as man coped with its whims and extremes.

And today, the desert is yielding. Jet planes zoom over the sands; irrigated farmlands thrive; desert mines supply uranium.

(CONTINUED ON BACK FLAP)

This Is the Desert

This Is The Desert

THE STORY OF AMERICA'S ARID REGION

by Phil Ault

ILLUSTRATED BY LEONARD EVERETT FISHER

DODD, MEAD & COMPANY · NEW YORK

To Frank, Ingrid and Bruce

Contents

This Is the Desert

1 From Dinosaurs to Jet Planes

The silvery jet fighter rolled with gathering momentum along the runway of Edwards Air Force Base in the Mojave desert of California. The major at the controls cast an experienced eye over the instrument panel. Satisfied that all was in order, he moved the controls deftly and the plane pointed its needle nose into the desert sky.

Sunshine glistened on the silver skin of the aircraft climbing swiftly to the west. Dark tails of exhaust trailed from the twin jet engines as they settled to their task of carrying the sleek, stub-winged fighter higher and higher. It was an exhilarating morning. Most mornings on the Mojave are.

1

Below lay the desert.

The day was several hours short of its peak, but already heat waves shimmered over the bed of the prehistoric dry lake at the air base. Whirlpools of dust danced across the hard-packed surface of the lake toward the rocket test range on the far side. The sandy plain, stretching in all directions, was dotted with the outstretched praying arms of Joshua trees. A scrubby growth of creosote bushes added a speckled greenish tinge to the bleak grayness of the soil.

The pilot checked his altitude. Ten thousand feet. A few moments later it was 20,000, then 30,000. From this height he could see the blue expanse of the Pacific Ocean stretching out to the west, just ahead of him.

Six miles below, the mountains formed a barrier between the desert and the ocean. Their western slopes toward the sea wore the deep green of forest and pasture. On the inland side the land lay in parched nakedness. This was where the desert began; on one side was water and abundant life, on the other the dryness of an intriguing, arid world.

The pilot swung the plane around to the east, still climbing. Men at the tracking station at Edwards were watching his flight on a radar screen and guiding him by radio. The man in the air and the technicians on the ground had a common goal: to bring the plane in over the desert base precisely on the ten-mile measured course in the sky. The U.S. Air Force was attempting to set a new world speed record.

As the jet fighter raced toward its base, the vast desert spread out ahead. Even from that altitude, there seems to be no end to it, stretching off to the east for hundreds of miles. Dry lake beds which have held little water for centuries dot the area. Ranges of stark, deeply creviced mountains with hardly a tree on their slopes break the monotony of the plain at intervals.

Hazy on the horizon rise the Panamints. In the gullies of these rock-strewn mountains men of an earlier generation hunted riches. They rarely found water but uncovered a glistening store of gold and silver. Prospectors roaming the region with their burros and a grubstake of bacon and beans struck it rich overnight. Others less fortunate died of thirst, their hands digging the sand in a frantic search for water. Only decaying ghost towns and collapsed mine shafts remain to show where thousands of miners once lived.

Beyond the Panamints to the east lies Death Valley. It is the loneliest place in America, and the lowest and hottest, where miles of the salt-encrusted desert floor are without vegetation and no animal can live. This is a place where the visitor must look up the mountainside 280 feet above him to see the mark of sea level.

Almost below the speeding pilot now was the stretch of alkaline-crusted desert. Two volunteer rescuers walked for nearly a month across its thirsty wastes in 1850 to save a tragic wagon train of gold-seeking emigrants who had blundered into Death Valley—one of the most remarkable rescues in American history.

3

On this same lonely area of desert, the sweating twenty-mule borax teams had hauled their heavy loads from Death Valley, urged along by a driver cracking a twenty-two-foot whip above their backs.

The jet pilot had no time for history just then, however. He was too busy making some of his own. Immediately ahead the shiny hangars and 15,000-foot runway of the desert test center were approaching.

On the ground a fast-action camera pointing straight up snapped a picture of the streaking plane. The pilot had his craft wide open, pouring every ounce of power into it that the two throbbing jets could produce. Another camera clicked, recording the end of the run. The jet had hurtled through ten miles of sky in less than thirty seconds. In less than half a minute the pilot had flown as far as covered wagons traveled on the desert in half a day.

The major's speed was so great that he needed a hundred miles to negotiate his turn and aim back at the course for a second run. He swung to the southeast across the desert and banked above Twentynine Palms. Near that oasis, now a booming small city, scientists have found pottery fragments and other evidence of life dating back perhaps 20,000 years.

Below on his left was Palm Springs, a luxurious resort town at the head of the Coachella Valley. Once this valley lay 300 feet deep beneath an ancient ocean. After that it was a sandy waste. In a rocky canyon nearby the tracks of dinosaurs and other prehistoric animals are clearly vis-

4

ible. Today the valley's date gardens and citrus groves hang heavy with luscious fruit because irrigation waters have revived the land.

The plane sped back toward its base, and a few minutes later skimmed in over the dry lake to a landing. The timing devices were checked and the two runs averaged. More than 1,400 miles an hour! A new world speed record. Another episode in the fabulous, many-faceted history of the western American desert had been written.

The western desert occupies approximately one-sixth of the United States, excluding Alaska. In this land of little water and immense space, history and nature have woven a unique pattern. Nowhere else in this country have men faced privation and peril in equally harsh surroundings.

In the far southwestern corner of the United States, where temperatures are high and rainfall skimpy, lies the most extreme desert—the real desert, as its inhabitants say. This bone-dry region includes parts of Southern California, Arizona, New Mexico and southern Nevada. Some parts of western Texas also are desert. To the north of this extremely dry region stretches the Great Basin desert between the Pacific coastal mountain range and the Rocky Mountains—bleak and monotonous but less violent, a land of sagebrush rather than cactus. The Great Basin desert covers most of Nevada, most of Utah and reaches north with dwindling intensity into Oregon, Idaho

5

and southwestern Wyoming. Within it lie the Great Salt Lake and the blazing white Bonneville salt flats, remnants of a gigantic ancient lake.

A different kind of desert country is found in the higher plateau of northern Arizona and New Mexico, and the southern corners of Utah and Colorado. This is the land of the Painted Desert, the Grand Canyon and the Navajo reservation—stony and arid, broken by deep canyons and fantastic rock formations.

All these deserts blend together into a gigantic whole, so that it is not easy to define where one part ends and the next begins. Over this vast region hangs the one compelling fact which unites these different terrains—lack of water.

A Hopi Indian in Arizona was attacking a sand dune with a bulldozer to clear the path for new construction. The blade of the earthmover laid bare a layer of rock. What the Indian saw surprised and puzzled him: huge footprints at intervals of several feet.

Work was halted while a geologist was summoned. He cleaned out the markings and recorded their size with a tape measure. "These are dinosaur tracks," he announced. "No doubt about it."

The desert holds many fascinating secrets in its dusty grip.

At some point in the dim past, perhaps about eighty million years ago, a lumbering creature weighing nearly thirty tons had clumped across this piece of ground. He

6

was more than forty feet in length, with a long curving neck and pinhead brain. As each of his giant feet came to rest on the soft surface, it made a five-toed mark.

The centuries passed. The muddy surface into which the dinosaur had stepped hardened into stone. The nearby hills eroded under the ceaseless beating of sunshine, wind and rain. The rocks became sand, and the millions of grains swirled and drifted until they formed large piles, or dunes. The dinosaur perished from the earth, and its footprints were buried beneath the sands. How many thousands of years they had been hidden there, until the bulldozer blade ripped away their covering, can only be guessed.

On the high desert, above 2,000 feet altitude, the night temperatures in winter sometimes fall below freezing. In midsummer a reading of 110 degrees is commonplace—and in Death Valley a maximum of 134 degrees has been recorded. Low humidity makes these temperatures more comfortable than they sound, however. Nights cool off sharply.

This is a land of contrasts, of extremes and contradictions. The horrifying stories of agony and death from thirst are true. Strangely enough, however, men have been known to drown on the desert miles from the nearest lake or stream. In spring the parched and dusty valleys, usually drab gray and tan, burst into a fantasy of colors as the desert wildflowers bloom in nature's spontaneous outburst of gaiety. Purple-hued mountains crisscross the land, providing spectacular scenic effects in the changing angles of the sunlight. Cactus is a desert trademark, yet in parts of the region no cactus can be found. The desert mountains still contain millions of dollars in gold ore, for which men once fought. Although the location of much of this gold is known, little effort is being made to mine it. The contradictions are many.

Here is solitude. The visitor's strongest impression is that of being engulfed in space. For miles nothing impedes his view of the dry earth spreading to the horizon beneath arching blue skies. The distances are even greater than they seem, in fact, because the clean, dry air plays an optical trick of making things appear closer than they are.

The desert is a place of fascination to geologists. In the gaunt, forbidding mountains enclosing Death Valley they have found examples of every geologic period. And even more intriguing than the clues to the desert's past is the way the animals and plants of today are able to survive and multiply in this arid land. Men cast adrift in the desert in summer can live only a relatively few hours without water, but the animals that call the desert their home function differently. The pocket mouse, desert fox, coyote, jackrabbit, varieties of lizards and snakes, the road runner and many others not only survive but flourish in the dry region.

The belief that the American desert is a land without vegetation is one of the most widely held misconceptions. Except in the alkaline dry lake beds, plant life of many varieties exists. This is the greatest difference between the American arid lands and some other great deserts of the world, especially the Sahara. Even in the sand dunes of the American desert, a few plants are able to get a foothold. Finding a gaily flowering plant surrounded by hundreds of yards of dry sand is a recurring delight for the desert traveler in springtime.

The western desert once was a frightening and almost unknown barrier between the eastern two-thirds of the United States and the far-distant Pacific coast. Travelers entered it with dread and prayed that they would cross it safely.

Today this same desert is regarded by many as a delightful place to live. It yields riches and performs services which its pioneers could never have imagined. A loose harness of highways and railroads has been thrown across the desert, binding the Pacific coast to the rest of the country. Civilization clusters along these routes. It is only a few steps, however, from the edge of the towns into almost barren soil. Men control the main paths with their automobiles, highways, watering systems and air conditioning, but the desert is not always humanity's willing servant. Away from the established tracks it remains a land of enchanted mystery and treachery where a man who wanders improperly prepared will perish.

Life is informal in this land where things move at a leisurely pace in the summer heat. The main buildings in the dusty, windswept hamlets are the gasoline station and the auto repair shack of corrugated iron next door. Here automobiles with water bags hanging from their bumpers —the badge of the desert motorist—pull in to refill before the fifty-mile trip to the next community. And here the wrinkled old-timers gather to spin tall tales about how they almost struck it rich while prospecting for gold, or to relate Death Valley Scotty's tall-tale adventures.

Woven into the desert's picturesque history are episodes of emigrants burning their covered wagons in a disastrous encounter with Death Valley, abandoned camels of the U. S. Army roaming the wastelands like ghosts, unsolved mysteries of early Indian communities, prospectors becoming rich overnight and lost mines whose hidden wealth still intrigues searchers.

The battle to check one of the strangest floods in history and erection of the world's highest dam . . . a mineral ignored by prospectors for years and now yielding an amazing array of useful products . . . air bases where there are 350 days of flying weather a year . . . explosion of the first atomic bomb . . . a seven-mile track along which rockets are fired at four times the speed of sound. These are the newest chapters of life on the desert.

Put these ancient and modern tales together, and the story of the American desert emerges. It is a rugged and adventurous tale, by turns funny, tragic, fascinating. The desert is the stage on which these events took place—and they happened only because of the uniqueness of their setting.

2 _What Is the Desert, Anyway?_

If asked to describe the great western desert of the United States, many Americans probably would say something like this, "The desert is a huge, hot and empty place where the heat is terrible, it never rains and hardly anything grows. About the only things that can live there are rattlesnakes."

Although partially correct, that popular conception is more false than true.

The distances _are_ gigantic. The desert _is_ extremely hot part of the year. Yet it can be bitterly cold. Usually it is dry and rainless. But even Death Valley, the driest place

in the western hemisphere, is sometimes swept by drench-
ing storms. As for living creatures, hundreds of thousands
of Americans reside on the desert in air-conditioned comfort and thousands more are flocking there every year. Yet
it is easy to travel scores of miles without seeing a house
or person.

What is the desert? Why does it exist and what lives
on it?

Some geographers say that a real desert begins when an
area receives less than ten inches of rainfall a year. New
York, for example, normally receives forty-one inches and
New Orleans fifty-nine. Rainfall in most of the American
desert is less than eight inches a year. Yuma, Arizona, gets
a mere four. Official readings in Death Valley some years
record less than an inch of precipitation and humidity
readings on some days are zero.

The main part of the American desert lies in the vast
arid basin between the Sierra Nevadas and the Rocky
Mountains 500 miles to the east. Rain-bearing winds
blowing inland from the Pacific Ocean strike the western
slope of the Sierra Nevadas. Since most of the clouds are
too low and heavy to cross the mountains, the lands east
of them receive only skimpy rainfall. They become desert.

The change from moist to arid lands is sharply drawn.
A motorist drives up into a pass over the Sierra Nevadas
from the Pacific coast through forests. A few miles later
he comes down the eastern slope into dry, barren desert.

Approaching from the east, the change is less remarkable. The grasslands of Texas blend into the sparser

range land of eastern New Mexico, the range land into semi-desert terrain. As the vegetation diminishes and watering places become rare, the land becomes what can be called true desert.

Water determines everything. If there is an abundant supply, the land blooms in profusion. Cities flourish in neon-lighted oases; farming areas yield large crops. Where there is no water, and this means most of the desert, the land is parched.

Only one important river system, the Colorado River and its tributaries, flows through the western desert of America. Others like the Mojave River start in the mountains, only to be swallowed up by the sands when they reach the valleys.

High winds and almost constant sunshine quickly evaporate most of the rain that falls. On the dry lake beds and valley slopes, the winds kick up whirlpools of dust. Thunderstorms striking the mountain tops send flash floods rampaging down the stream beds, drowning anyone foolish enough to camp there. A few hours later the streams are dry again. The thirsty soil has gobbled every drop.

The fact that moisture-loving dinosaurs lived in this barren region in ancient times seems baffling at first glance. These mammoth, slow-moving creatures enjoyed splashing in rivers and forest swamps, and eating the lush green plants that crowded the water's edge. How could a dinosaur live in a land where the ground is hard-packed sand and gravel, its only vegetation a sprinkling of low, dry bushes, sage and cactus?

The answer is that when the dinosaurs lived, the region modern men know as the American desert was not desert at all. It was dotted with large inland lakes. Parts of what is now the western United States lay hundreds of feet under the ocean. The Gulf of California reached a hundred miles northward from its present boundaries, perhaps all the way to the San Gorgonio pass southeast of Los Angeles. Forests of evergreens covered the land, rising nearly a hundred feet above the fern-covered ground. The climate was moist and warm.

Many changes have taken place in these lands since the dinosaur made his tracks. The land was shaken by earthquakes of an intensity far beyond what the world experiences today. The floor of the ocean rose above the surface and became land as the waters receded. Muddy sediment that had settled to the floor of the ocean hardened into rock, limestone and sandstone. The bony remains of fish and the intricate patterns of coral were trapped in this stiffening ooze. Volcanoes were born and for thousands of years spewed their lava and ashes across the land; parts of the desert today are covered with harsh reddish lava.

Then the ice age came. Sheets of glacial ice spread down over the northern part of the United States, changing the landscape and turning the weather frigid. After thousands of years this era passed, too. The glaciers retreated. The waters running off from them drained into the low spots, creating inland lakes.

Gradually the climate dried out. The mighty range of Sierra Nevadas, which rose during the chaotic period of

15

earthquakes, became a rain barrier. The desert began to form.

With no more glacial waters to feed them and rainfall blocked by the mountains, the inland lakes evaporated. Some of them left flat, salt-laden beds to mark their sites, and to be mined today for use in modern industry. Rogers Dry Lake at Edwards Air Force Base was formed in this manner.

The drying-out process has been continuous for many centuries, and the past has left many reminders of its actions. Oftentimes they are unique and awesomely picturesque, lending an air of mystery and allure to the desert region. Beach lines of the ancient lakes and seas are visible at several places, stained deep into the rock dozens of feet above the present valley levels. The lake that once covered much of Utah had a water level a thousand feet above that of the present Salt Lake, as shown by the shoreline marks on the surrounding slopes.

Erosion through the ages has formed highly colored gorges, the most famous of which is the breathtaking Grand Canyon. Fossil remains of mastodons, antelopes, horses and birds, found in the clay bottom of Lake Manix in the Mojave, intrigue geologists. The Petrified Forest in eastern Arizona is a treasure house of prehistoric trees. Once living and now turned to stone, they were laid bare by the quirks of earthquake upheavals.

In this "land where there isn't enough water" plants, animals and men must fight to survive and conquer their surroundings. Human beings have never been able to adapt their bodies to endure without water. We belong to the legion of *water wasters*. We consume large amounts of liquid which then escapes from our bodies in perspiration and other ways; our bodies cannot store water, as the camel can. A scientist has estimated that a man of average weight walking eight hours a day on the Colorado desert in July should drink about three gallons of liquid a day to retain his weight.

Animals of the desert are *water savers*. Through the centuries their bodies have been altered from those of their cousins in damper climates. They have acquired the skill of finding tiny particles of water in odd places and hoarding in their bodies the moisture they find. Some desert rodents can live their entire lives without drinking a single drop of water!

They do so because they have the ability to create water of their own through processes of chemical change. Hydrogen and oxygen are extracted from the food they eat and combined into water within their bodies. By instinctive practices of conservation, such as spending the daylight hours away from the sun in burrows or under rocks, they can sustain their lives with this self-generated water. A person can hike or drive across the desert in daylight during summer and say, "Why, there isn't a living thing to be seen!"

Night falls and the desert comes alive. Creatures which have spent the hot hours under cover come forth to prowl for food.

The tiniest of all the desert mammals is the lively pocket mouse, a creature of the night hardly bigger than a walnut. Yet he can leap two or three feet in a single bound if his safety depends upon it. He is called the pocket mouse not because he is pocket size, or less, but because he has a pair of cheek pouches in which he collects plant seeds. These he hauls to his underground nest for his winter food supply. His tiny front feet move with amazing swiftness as he picks up the seeds and stuffs them into his pockets.

From these dry seeds he creates enough water to keep himself alive. He protects himself from the daytime heat by crawling down into his hole, then plugging it with sand. When the winds blow, more sand drifts into the hole above this plug and wipes away all traces of his hiding place. Nature's mysterious alarm clock rings when the sun goes down. The mouse pushes his sensitive nose up through the sand, clears it away with a few flicks of his quick feet and emerges for a night of scampering around the desert.

Among his companions on this foraging are dozens of different animals. There are desert foxes, coyotes, bobcats, kangaroo rats, gophers, even occasional deer in certain parts of the desert. Rattlesnakes like to crawl onto the shoulders of the roads after nightfall. Lizards abound, darting from rock to rock. Jackrabbits with ears almost as big as a donkey's leap across the dry lands at an astounding clip.

The lizards are the most frequently seen. More than

fifty varieties live in the American desert, many of which dart about busily during the daylight hours.

Among the most colorful lizards is the scaly, rugged chuckawalla. He is a big fellow some sixteen inches long, half of which is tail, with sharp teeth that can inflict a nasty bite. The chuckawalla does not have to use his teeth in self-defense very often, however. He has a much more distinctive way of confounding his enemies. When frightened, he slithers into a crevice between rocks. If some other animal or a human attempts to pull him out of this refuge, the chuckawalla inflates his lungs. He becomes so enlarged that his leathery body fills the entire crevice, making it impossible for his foe to dislodge him.

Tortoises are frequently seen, even in the sand and gravel of mid-desert. Nearly a foot in length, the hard-shelled creatures move slowly and eat plant life. They are a nuisance to homesteaders who grow melons and other edibles. Whenever possible the tortoise will drink large quantities of water, on which it can survive for a prolonged period.

Every desert species has its deadly enemies. The pocket mouse must be constantly on the alert lest a desert fox or an owl should gobble him up. The coyote tries to kill the jackrabbit and ground squirrels live in fear of the snakes. Life is harsh and difficult. Every creature must take care of itself by quickness of foot, ability to strike back or protective coloration that enables it to blend itself with the ground, the rocks or the vegetation.

Poison is used by a few animals to protect themselves.

19

Among those employing this weapon is the Gila monster, an ugly lizard which looks like a creature left over from prehistoric times. Growing to a maximum length of two feet, it crawls along with five-toed feet. Its body is covered with a hard, bead-like substance that reminds those who see it of a woman's beaded purse. Its favorite food is raw eggs. When it bites, the Gila monster spurts poison through grooves in its teeth into the wound. The poison affects the victim's nerves, but fortunately laboratory experiments indicate that the creature cannot deliver enough in one bite to kill an adult human being.

The desert rattlesnakes are more deadly. Their bites can kill a man. Those who travel off the beaten path are well advised to carry a snakebite kit, although rattlesnakes are far less numerous on the American desert than popularly believed. They are most frequently seen in the spring. Most of them will strike only when they believe themselves in danger. Desert visitors who use ordinary caution need not worry unduly about rattlesnakes, but they should keep their eyes open. Anyone who carelessly puts his hand under a bush without first poking with a stick, or walks along a roadside at night without a flashlight is asking for trouble.

Curiously, while rattlesnakes are numerous in certain desert regions, including the cactus forest of Arizona, some of them cannot stand the summer heat. These will hide under rocks and vegetation during daylight. Some species will die if exposed to the hot summer sun for a short time.

Around the desert the traveler will find Sidewinder Wells, Sidewinder Springs, Sidewinder Mines and other landmarks bearing this odd name. These are named after the sidewinder rattlesnake. This venomous creature travels by looping itself sideways, rather than pulling itself straight ahead as most snakes do. This motion, which leaves a trail like a string of J's tied together, enables the sidewinder to pull himself through soft sand. Most rattlesnakes prefer rocks and hard-packed surfaces.

Insects, spiders and scorpions are numerous in dry country. Only two of the many species of scorpion are poisonous, but the bites of these two can be fatal. Black widow spiders also can inflict deadly bites. However, the great majority of desert insects are harmless, more notable for their ability to survive almost without moisture than to inflict damage.

The desert is home, too, for many kinds of birds. Even in the barren regions of Death Valley more than 230 species of birds have been identified. Many are only visitors, stopping off for a few days or weeks on their annual migrations between warm and cold climates.

Of all the birds the most amusing and perhaps the cruelest is the road runner. This unique bird grows nearly two feet long, about half of which is his tail. Sometimes this almost drags on the ground; on other occasions it points up into the air in a jaunty manner. Atop the road runner's head is a black topknot which stands straight up when he is alarmed.

The road runner prefers to pursue his quarry by running at a swift, clumsy-looking pace across the desert. He can fly, but when he touches earth again it is in a running landing, his feet churning to carry him forward. He will eat just about anything that moves, if he can grab it in his long beak, no matter if his prey is a snake or some other creature too big for his stomach to handle at one sitting. He bustles about, carrying the dinner in his beak until his stomach is ready for it. His appetite is ravenous and his hunting instincts keen. Road runners have been known to leap into the air and catch small birds on the wing. Often they slam their victims against a rock to kill them, then go ahead with their feast.

The many animals and birds of the desert find both food and shelter in the extensive vegetation of the region. Often thought of as a place "where hardly anything grows," the desert holds an amazing wealth of plant life.

Viewed from above, the desert has a mottled appearance of green and tan, as though a person has sprinkled a handful of leaves in a sandbox. Each plant is surrounded by a barren circle of sandy clay or rocky soil. Grass, shrubs and small trees form a solid carpet of green only around the occasional streams or water holes where moisture is plentiful.

This spacing between plants is the secret of desert greenery. Nature in her delicately balanced way sees to it that there are only as many plants as the skimpy water supply can support. Only the sturdiest of the seedlings survive the rigorous growing conditions. Thus the plants which do reach maturity are the strongest of their kind.

Their roots reach out long distances for the life-giving

moisture. Some plants send long fingers as much as fifty feet below the earth's surface. Others have intricate shallow root networks, spreading fanlike just under the surface. The bare earth around each plant covers its root system. No other growth can get a toehold in the space because the established plant has its feelers out for all the water that falls or drains into its private kingdom. In places the desert plants are spaced so evenly that they suggest the appearance of a landscaped garden.

Another distinctive feature the traveler notices about desert plant growth is its symmetry. Most plants are equally bushy on all sides. The open spaces around them allow the abundant sunshine to strike the bushes and trees from every direction. Few plants languish in the shadows of others.

If a single feature can be said to distinguish desert plants as a whole from their relatives in damper climates, it is their prickly surface. Thorns, needles, stickers are present in great abundance. These are part of the plants' water-absorption systems. Some botanists suggest that these spiny stickers also provide shade for the plants, like a slat house. Whatever the reason, handle with care!

The seeds of desert plants are enduring. After being scattered from their parent growths by the wind or by animals, they may lie dormant in the dry ground for a long time. When a rain comes, even a relatively few drops, the seeds come to life with surprising speed. Soon the desert takes on a fresh, bright green cast.

Since many of the plants bear gay flowers, the desert is

often splashed with riotous color. Larkspur, lupine, poppies, primroses, desert asters, verbena and a score of other wildflowers bloom in a profusion of yellows, reds, whites, blues and purples. The life cycle of each plant is brief, only a few days in many cases. They die in the heat and their seeds lie idle until the next spell of moisture comes along.

Full-grown plants of the sturdier species have a knack for surviving during long dry spells. They may wither and look as though they have died, but let a little water come their way and they perk up in a hurry.

The most frequently seen desert plant is the creosote bush. Sometimes this is called greasewood because of the shiny surface of its leaves. The odor of creosote is very noticeable in this sturdy shrub, which is especially adept at surviving draught. Botanists have on record one instance on the Mojave desert where not a drop of rain fell for thirty-two months and the interval between effective rains was much longer. The creosote bushes in the area looked withered and dead. Shortly after the first good rain, however, new leaves sprouted and the plants became fresh and vigorous.

Like the animals, desert shrubs have adapted themselves to the dryness. Nature has given them special means of drawing in water and protecting themselves against evaporation. Some plants can store water supplies in their trunks or roots; others are notable for their small leaf surfaces to reduce evaporation. Resin on stems and leaves that are hairy, woolly or covered with a waxy surface help hold the water that has been absorbed from the air.

The mesquite tree, often only a large shrub, is a common sight on the desert. How a tree that sometimes has a trunk several feet in circumference can grow in places where so little moisture exists is a source of wonder. Desert men know that wherever a mesquite tree stands there must be water near, even though none is apparent on the surface.

The pods of the mesquite, and the beans they contain, are an important food source for the Indians of the southwest. The U.S. Cavalry in New Mexico used to pay three cents a pound for mesquite beans. The pods of one variety of mesquite have spiral markings and are known as screwbeans.

Ask anybody to name the first plant that comes to mind when he thinks of the desert. Almost certainly he will reply, "Cactus." These spiny, leafless plants have become the symbol of the American desert. They are rarely found anywhere but on the deserts of the western United States. In fact they are not seen everywhere in our own dry lands, but primarily in Arizona.

The most spectacular of the many cactus types is the giant saguero, rising to heights of nearly fifty feet and pointing its spiny arms from its main trunk toward the skies with primitive dignity. The green skin of the saguero is pleated like an accordion, each vertical indentation being partially filled with olive-green pulp. This is the saguero's water storage system. During damp intervals it collects water on which it lives during the hot, dry months. Gradually the arms of the saguero shrivel during drought periods; with the coming of rain they bulge until the skin is tight.

Indian women learned how to obtain nourishment for their families from this giant cactus. From the tips of the long green arms reaching toward the sky, Papago Indian women pull down the clusters of red fruit with long sticks. The meaty center of the raw fruit is eaten, the rinds thrown away. The juice can be drained off for drinking, or boiled down to syrup. The pulp is boiled and strained through loose-woven baskets, then spread out to dry; then it can be stored for later eating or made into jam. Even the saguero seeds have their uses as food—either fed to the chickens or roasted, ground into powder and eaten in a mixture with sugar as a delicacy.

The birds know what a handy water source the saguero is. Woodpeckers drill holes in its pulp to obtain moisture. After the scars have healed the elf owls and other small birds move into the holes for nesting. Some birds gather broken cactus spines as materials for their nests, or build their nests right onto the trunk of a cactus, using the spines as a framework.

Desert travelers suffering from thirst have found life-saving water in the plump, thorny barrel cactus, so named because it looks somewhat like a barrel. When the cactus is cut open, a spongy mass is revealed. This can be beaten with a stick until a considerable amount of moisture oozes

out. That peculiar desert confection, cactus candy, also comes from the interior of the barrel cactus.

Others in this leafless plant family include the organ pipe cactus, the pincushion, the prickly pear, whose clusters of green paddles often provide a hiding place for the nests of wood rats, and the jumping cholla. The latter gets its name from the popular belief that its needle-sharp spines jump at a passer-by. They don't, but the merest touch will bury them painfully into the skin.

Two more shrubs and trees deserve mention in the desert's gallery of fantastic plants. These are the yucca and the ocotillo. The yucca is a small tree whose crown of pointed leaves slightly resembles a palm tree. It grows as high as twenty feet and produces clusters of white blooms in the spring.

The big brother of this common yucca is the Joshua tree. Rising thirty feet or more, this tree has a fascinating array of fuzzy arms uplifted to the sky as though in prayer. Pioneers seeing this tree thought of the Biblical prophet, Joshua, and jokingly applied his name to the tree. The name came into common usage and now is officially accepted in botany books. The Joshua tree grows in "forest" formations, scattered over hundreds of square miles of the Mojave desert.

The word ocotillo in Spanish means "little pine," although this weird desert plant is not a pine at all. It sends numerous long thorny stems radiating into the air from a central root, waving like wands in the wind. These are also called coachwhips. Most of the time the stems are dry and thorny, but when a rain comes they are covered briefly with tiny leaves. An ocotillo plant may burst into leaf several times a year, depending upon the moisture in the air. Clusters of scarlet flowers blossom on the tips of their naked stems.

Although palm trees are frequently shown in drawings of the desert, these lovely spreading trees are found only in the hot, lower desert areas such as the Coachella valley.

Truly the desert is one of the most fascinating places in the world to study animal and plant life. Those who travel slowly enough to look around, or better yet, take time to walk across the desert floor, will find a botany laboratory and a menagerie exceptional in character. Before them is spread a marvelous demonstration of how living things can adapt themselves to prosper in a land where living is difficult and survival belongs to those who fight the hardest.

3 Before the White Men Came

The desert plateau of western New Mexico rolls on and on like the sea. Here and there the expanse is broken by an island of rock, its perpendicular walls rising suddenly from the sandy plain. These are the mesas.

A traveler who turns south from the main transcontinental highway, U.S. 66, and goes fifteen miles out into the open country sees before him such a gray rock mass. Surrounded by sun-baked desert, this forbidding island towers straight up from the plain 350 feet and spreads over an area of seventy acres.

At first there seems no way to climb the isolated outcrop, whose walls are so sheer that they overhang in places.

The rock faces are scarred by deep crevices. Around the base clusters a mass of debris broken off by the erosion of centuries. The top of the sandstone pile is a flat tableland.

Closer examination reveals a trail. Those who climb it must scramble up a dent in the cliff, fitting toes and fingers into ancient cavities. At the more difficult points they are aided by ladders.

Arriving at the top, the visitor can look out over the cactus-studded plain spreading in all directions, drab and lonely. Perched on the lofty plateau before him, isolated from the desert world around it by the perpendicular walls of the mesa, stands an ancient pueblo. This is Acoma, the sky city, the oldest continuously inhabited town in America.

Acoma is a living link with the desert's long inhabited past, dating back so many centuries that nobody can be sure when it was built on its rocky pinnacle. When the Spanish explorers came north across the desert from Mexico in 1540, they found Indians living atop this wind-swept rock very much as their descendants live there today. Indians had inhabited the mighty rock outcrop for several hundred years before another group of Spaniards established the first white man's settlement in North America in 1565, at Saint Augustine, Florida. Acoma was an ancient town by the time the Pilgrims landed on the faraway eastern coast of America in 1620.

Situated though it is in a position of grandeur, Acoma as seen through the white man's eyes is a dreary, unattractive village. There is no blade of grass, tree or shrub to give a warming touch of green to the dull gray rock. The sun-bleached dwellings of adobe and stacked flat stones blend so well with the rock of the mesa that they seem almost a part of it. Winds swirl the pulverized sand through the village plaza and along the rows of connected houses rising three stories and built in a setback arrangement like giant stairsteps with hand-hewn ladders leading to the upper floors. Existence in this stark setting always has been harsh. The ancient Indians came here to live only in order to escape their desert enemies.

Ancient as Acoma is, the lore of that community tells of another Indian settlement that existed before it, and from which the first people of Acoma came. This is the story of the Enchanted Mesa.

To the north of Acoma three miles there rises another mesa, even higher, steeper and more forbidding. This is Katzimo. A thousand years or more ago, so the legend runs, an Indian community lived happily on its barren top, their houses built of adobe hauled up from the plain 430 feet below. The people of Katzimo, some six hundred of them, cultivated fields of corn and beans in the valley nearby, descending the single trail, a sloping rock face in which toeholds had been hacked, each morning and climbing up again to their pueblo at night. At this high altitude they were safe from marauding bands of warriors.

At the harvest season one summer, the entire village population descended to the valley to gather the crops. Only three women remained on the mesa, one of whom was sick. An enormous storm struck the area while the

harvesting was in progress. A flash flood rolled through the valley, and the ladder rock fell onto the plain with a thundering crash. The only path from the ground to the mesa top had been destroyed. Those who had remained on top faced starvation; one of the women threw herself over the cliff.

Mournfully the people turned away from their rock and went to Acoma. There they started the town which still exists. They lived in fear of Katzimo and never went there again. It became known as the Enchanted Mesa.

This story was passed on to the white men by the people of Acoma and was published in magazines. Many people scoffed at it. Just a myth, they said. An eastern professor, intending to prove that the Enchanted Mesa had never been occupied, had himself hauled to the top of the rock plateau in a bosun's chair. He spent two hours there and came down convinced that nobody had ever been on the top before.

Such disbelief angered the white men who had spent many years among the Indians. They were positive that the legend had basis in fact. Frederick W. Hodge of the Bureau of American Ethnology set out to prove the professor wrong. Using an extension ladder built in sections, he and his companions made their way to the top of Katzimo.

Centuries of rain, wind and sun had disintegrated the ancient houses, but they searched and found an assortment of stone axes, arrowheads, fragments of earthen cooking pots, shell beads and other evidence that humans had in truth resided on the lofty peak. The photographer, A. C. Vroman, took pictures of the discoveries to prove the point. The mesa was indeed enchanted.

The pueblo Indians of the sky city of Acoma have managed to live on the unyielding desert for centuries. It is no easy existence.

All building materials had to be gathered from the desert plains and ravines below and hauled up the precipitous mesa trail in baskets. An agricultural people, the Acomans coaxed skimpy crops from fields in the surrounding desert wherever they could find a little moisture. At night, and in times of peril, they shut themselves up in their towering dwelling place as in a fortress.

After the white man had established his control over the desert country, and the murderous raids of warlike tribes had ceased, the people of Acoma began to spend more of their time on the desert plain, until today most of them live a large part of the year "down below." Their aged village on the mesa always has some residents, however, because the pull of tribal custom is immense, and at festival times the sky city is heavily populated.

The most impressive sight atop the rock is the church of San Esteban Re, the largest mission church in the southwest. The Indians built it under direction of Spanish priests more than 300 years ago. As the visitor examines the walls, nearly ten feet thick at the base, and the huge beams, he finds it difficult to realize that these had to be cut in the hills thirty miles away and brought across the plain by hand. There were no beasts of burden. Even the dirt for the church cemetery had to be hauled up the trail in baskets by the patient Indian desert dwellers.

Most of the early Indians braved the heat and dryness of the desert not through a taste for adventure, but because they were pushed onto it by stronger, more warlike tribes. As a result of these primitive struggles the weakest, least aggressive people ended up on the barren land their stronger foes did not want. But once established on the desert, these nomads found that it had advantages—a warm, dry climate, plentiful dry firewood from dead bushes in many places and fibers from plants for making clothing. In the high desert they found caves for shelter. They learned that the sticky adobe clay could be molded and patted into comfortable dwellings. And they kept themselves alive by eating the mesquite beans, seeds of the chia sage, the young shoots of the century plant and, in the desert mountains, by harvesting pine nuts and acorns. The fruit of the saguero cactus also became part of their diet. This was a sparse existence, but it satisfied these early desert peoples. All the foods on which they survived are still to be found on the desert today.

Their overwhelming problem was water—just as it is for desert dwellers today. Since these ancient farmers lacked the tools and skill for digging deep wells, they lived close to such water holes, springs and streams as they could find. They scratched out fields with primitive stick and stone tools, and offered elaborate ceremonial prayers

for rain so their crops would ripen. Traditional rain dances are still performed by some desert Indian tribes, with almost as much fervor as their ancestors displayed.

About the time that Christ lived, the Indians learned the art of raising corn. As the centuries passed they acquired more skills and learned to use the bow and arrow. Gradually they began to build pueblos, such as Acoma and Katzimo, or community dwellings, like the cliff houses which a thousand years later are still standing in remote corners of New Mexico and Arizona.

The construction of these multiple-roomed clay and

stone buildings in the rock cliffs was a remarkable feat of primitive skill. The cliff dwellers had no knowledge of metals and their tools were made of stone and wood. They knew nothing about the wheel. They had no animals to haul their materials. Everything used in these structures had to be dragged up into the hollowed-out cliffs along difficult trails. When they wanted to cut a building block, it had to be done by the tiresome process of hitting stone against stone.

Yet their masonry work was amazingly good. Stones were cut neatly and matched for size. The more elaborate buildings had contrasting bands of colored stone for decoration. The masons built walls with precisely squared corners, buildings several stories high and even circular watch towers.

At the Chaco Canyon National Monument in Northwestern New Mexico stand the remains of fourteen Indian pueblo communities. The largest of these is called Pueblo Bonito. Through the study of tree rings, scientists know that construction work here went on for 300 years, from 828 to 1130 A.D. Now long deserted, this was a thriving, bustling town at the peak of its strength, more than 400 years before Christopher Columbus sailed to discover the New World.

Why were these homes abandoned? Did lack of water ruin the Indians' fields and force them to move elsewhere? Was it the invasion of the Apache and Navajo tribes from the north that forced the peaceful pueblo dwellers to flee southward? Whatever the reason, the cliff houses and many of the pueblos in more open country had been abandoned for more than a century before the Spanish explorers came to the desert.

Further south in the flat, sandy desert of the Gila River valley a different race of Indians have left evidence of their existence in a land where it was difficult to survive. These are the Hohokem, an Indian word meaning "those who have gone."

Skilled as builders and ditch diggers, they dug irrigation ditches from the rivers to water the dried-out land and raised crops of corn, beans, pumpkins and cotton. Considering their primitive tools, their irrigation work was excellent. It was a forerunner of the elaborate water distribution system which exists today in the same area, between Phoenix and Tucson, Arizona.

The most remarkable remnant of the vanished Hohokem civilization is an adobe ruin called Casa Grande, standing on the open desert south of the Gila River near Florence, Arizona. The visitor who comes to this crumbling ruin sees an eerie reminder of a whole people who have disappeared from the earth. Scientists have calculated that it was built about 1350 A.D., two centuries before the white man, but they know little more about the purpose and history of this building than did the first white visitors who found its deserted hulk 400 years ago.

Casa Grande stands four stories high with walls four feet thick at the base. No rocks are to be found in the sandy region, and the structure is built of an adobe mud called *caliche*. A mud house more than 600 years old! Because the weathering of many centuries is weakening the ruin, the federal government has built a protective metal shed over it.

Why did the Hohokem need such a primitive sky-scraper? What has become of the people who built it? The Hohokem are truly "those who have gone." They have left no written records and no tribal lore passed down from one generation to the next.

Among the mysteries of Casa Grande are the calendar holes. In the east wall of the ground floor is a hole about an inch and a half in diameter which penetrates all the way through the four-foot thickness. On a wall inside the building is an identical hole, opening into the central downstairs room.

On March 7 each year, at 6:53 a.m., a beam of morning sunlight shines through the long outer hole and strikes the inner wall where the second hole has been cut. Clearly it was designed so this sunbeam would shine on through the second hole, into the central room. A slight settling in the outer wall has occurred, however, and the sunbeam now misses the inner hole by a fraction of an inch. The same thing happens at the same minute each October 7. This must have been an ingenious astronomical timekeeper by a people who had no clocks.

At many places in the desert, from California all the way eastward to New Mexico, there are thousands of Indian inscriptions on rocks. These remain a mystery. Some have been painted and drawn on the surface, known as pictographs. Others, called petroglyphs, are engraved in the rock. Some look like crude animals, others are circles, whorls, crisscross patterns and herringbone designs.

Investigators have many theories, but no complete answer to these writings. Some of the symbols were trail markers, undoubtedly. Others may have pointed to water. This much we do know: these rock writings do not represent a formal written language, like the hieroglyphics of ancient Egypt.

The Indians of the open desert were rugged. The hot, dry miles of barren land seem to have held few fears for these ancient ones. They walked everywhere on the desert and wore trails which are still to be seen. Three main trunk systems of Indian trails stretch across the Colorado desert westward from Arizona to the coastal mountains of California.

One of these runs almost parallel with the route of U.S. Highway 60–70. Generally it lies a mile or more north of the cement highway, clinging to higher ground where the footing is firmer. At the eastern end of this ancient foot-path, close to the Colorado River, is another of the desert's unsolved Indian mysteries.

About twenty-five years ago a pilot flying along the Colorado near Blythe was searching for a possible emergency landing field. He looked down from 5,000 feet and to his surprise saw the immense figure of a man stretched out on the desert mesa. Circling lower, he detected other crude figures of a four-legged animal and a coiled snake. Landing at Blythe, he organized a search party which, driving across the desert to the landmarks he had noted, found the figures.

That these are prehistoric in origin there is no doubt. But what do they represent and why were they placed in this lonely spot? After a quarter century of puzzling, the experts still have not found the answer.

Ancient tribesmen created these giant figures by raking or brushing the small stones and gravel into ridges. These form the outline of the designs. There is a dark coating of desert "varnish" on the pebbles, while the soil beneath them is a light, sunbaked clay color. Thus the area scraped clean stands out in sharp contrast to the dark stony desert around it.

The figure of the man which caught the pilot's attention looks like the kind of people boys and girls in kindergarten draw. The arms and legs are long and thin. From above, the man appears to be lying flat on his back. A giant fellow he is, too, measuring ninety-five feet long. On higher mesas additional sets of figures were found, in each case a man, an animal and a coiled serpent. The largest man of all is 167 feet long.

Recently the high school students of Blythe volunteered their time to restore these mysterious figures. Visitors had thoughtlessly kicked the stone borders until they were losing their shape. Work crews of boys and girls went at the job with rakes, brooms and wheelbarrows. They scraped the figures clean of debris and renewed the outlines. The loosened stones of the ridges were turned over so that the dark weathered or "varnished" side was upright again. The citizens of Blythe contributed funds for a wire mesh fence to protect the figures.

Thus the mysteries of ancient life on the American desert pile up. These giant figures, the adobe tower at Casa Grande, the abandoned cliff houses, the Enchanted Mesa, the rocks covered with undeciphered writing: these and other relics are reminders of peoples who lived in America for hundreds of years before the first Europeans dared to cross the Atlantic. We have built our civilization on top of theirs while inheriting little of their knowledge or traditions. The only thing we share has been a common challenge to bend the harsh and arid desert to our needs.

The Indian tribes of the desert regions today are a peaceful remnant of the earlier warlike days. They have taken on many of the ways of modern civilization without losing entirely the religious beliefs and ceremonies of their ancestors. The men wear overalls and the women cotton dresses instead of their native garb. Canned goods line the pueblo shelves. Washing machines are to be seen in many of the dirt-floored huts. The children are learning English in government schools.

Largest of all the tribes are the Navajos. Oil and, more recently, uranium have been found on their reservation. Large sums in royalties are paid to them for land leases, and their poverty, once extreme, is disappearing.

Many young Navajo men served in World War II, fill-ing a unique purpose in the U. S. Army. Since the Navajo language is unlike anything known in Europe or Asia, these desert Indians could talk openly on combat radios without fear of giving away secrets to the enemy. They delivered orders by walkie-talkie radio in Navajo, then translated into English for their commanding officers. This was faster and safer than a code.

But centuries of habit and tradition cannot be changed overnight. Six-sided log houses and the forked-stick Indian *hogans* of brush and mud can be seen on the desert reservations today. The door of each *hogan* opens to the east, as tribal custom decrees, and the belief that a *hogan* must be abandoned after someone has died in it still exists.

The desert Indian tribes cling to their ceremonial dances, to which visitors often are admitted. In these intricate ceremonies the Indians pray for rain, good crops and other blessings as much desired today in the arid land as by their ancestors. Those who watch their dances feel a primitive throb of excitement in the rhythmic beating of the drums, stomping of feet, and rustling of shells.

The white man may not fully understand the symbolic meanings, but those who know the desert know that these rites are ancient ties to the past—in a land where nature's challenge has changed but little over the years.

4 The First White Men Arrive

The Spanish army of Don Francisco Vasquez de Coronado had been on the march northward from Mexico for many months in the year 1540 and had grown weary. It was a proud army and fierce in battle. But it was also a hungry army.

For days it had been moving across the desert in what is now southeastern Arizona. A great cloud of dust engulfed the expedition, stirred up by the horses of the *cabelleros,* the feet of the infantrymen and Indian servants, the pack mules and sheep which followed in the train. Watering places were few. The desert heat shimmered unmercifully upon the steel breastplates and helmets of the soldiers. They had been on the march much longer than their leaders had anticipated and their stocks of food were running low.

Day after day the soldiers and their followers peered to the horizon, searching for their goal. Although the Spanish army was short of food, it was rich in expectations— expectations of great cities glittering with gold and silver and pearls, so wealthy that the women wore belts of pure gold and the doors of their tall houses were encrusted with jewels.

Coronado's army was, in fact, searching for the land of Cibola and its fabled Seven Cities of Gold. Instead, all they had found was desert—thirst and hunger and seemingly endless wastelands in which no men lived.

That the Cities of Gold existed somewhere in this dusty region the Spaniards had no doubt. Walking with them, clad in the sandals and cassock of his faith, was a Franciscan priest who had actually seen the greatest of these cities. At least he said he had, and in those days, a half century after Columbus when the wonders of the new world still were unfolding, nobody had reason to doubt his word.

Fray Marcos de Niza, the priest, had gone north from Mexico two years earlier on a scouting expedition into the desert. He returned safely to Mexico City after many adventures with wondrous tales about the land which he called Cibola.

"The greatest of the seven cities is larger than this City

46

of Mexico," he said as he described its riches to the Viceroy. "I have seen it myself from a short distance."

The Viceroy and Coronado, a wealthy young Spaniard, put up their own money to finance an army that would go north across the desert and seize these riches, just as the Spaniards had conquered and looted Mexico. The prize was a tantalizing one, well worth the hardships and heavy costs of an expedition. The Spaniards were brave, ruthless and greedy for gold.

The lands into which the army marched were virtually unknown to the white man. What is now the United States was only a huge blank space on the existing maps. One of these showed the Atlantic and Pacific Oceans as being only a few miles apart. Coronado had another ambition on his trip, to discover a sea passage between the two oceans, but this was secondary to his main desire—treasure.

So matters stood when Coronado's army one day captured three Indians skulking in the hills and learned from them that their city lay only a short march ahead. Cibola at last!

Its spirits revived by the nearness of the goal, Coronado's army advanced through Zuni canyon in the western edge of New Mexico, about sixty miles south of present-day Gallup. They saw smoke signals and Indian scouts watching them from a distance. Then, making a turn in the canyon, they saw the city.

Their hearts sank. Could this be the famous metropolis of Cibola—this dingy mud pueblo? Hardly a thousand persons lived here in squalor, eking out a bare existence. Rarely in history has a dream been so thoroughly shattered.

Fray Marcos, the imaginative teller of tall tales, hung far back in the rear of the army, but even his holy garments could not protect him from the blistering tongue-lashing of the disappointed soldiers. Five months of hardship for this!

About two hundred Zunis were drawn up outside the pueblo awaiting the Spaniards. Resenting this intrusion of their desert home, they made a ceremonial line of colored meal and indicated that the invaders should not cross it. Other warriors stood on the terraces of the adobe houses, waiting.

An advance party of Spaniards crossed the line. Immediately they were met by a volley of arrows. Coronado, clad in his golden armor, came forward, making signs of peace, but he too drew a shower of arrows.

The commander shouted "Advance!" and the Spaniards surged forward. Against the Indians' bows and arrows the armored warriors fired their primitive guns, called arquebuses, and crossbows. They hurled lances and slashed at the Indians with their swords. The scuffling and struggling on the dry, hot desert ground kicked up a cloud of dust which engulfed the battle scene.

The Indians retreated to the pueblo and hurriedly climbed up the ladders to the terraces. But luck was with the attackers, because in their haste the Indians failed to drag up one of the ladders. Coronado led the charge to capture it. From above the Indians hurled rocks and dropped large boulders, one of which hit Coronado and almost crushed him. An arrow pierced his foot and he was knocked unconscious.

Finally the Spaniards climbed the ladder, leaped onto the terrace and subdued the Indians. They found neither gold nor silver in their search of the pueblo, but they did find something that pleased them almost as much for the moment—an abundance of corn, beans and turkeys. For the first time in days the Spanish army had a good meal.

The white man had arrived on the American desert, laying a trail of blood and plunder.

Coronado was determined to find gold in this barren land if any was to be found. These first white men were driven not by the urge to explore the desert, or to colonize new lands, but to find treasure they could carry away. When they sensed riches in the offing, Spanish soldiers could endure great hardships cheerfully. In many ways the desert reminded them of the dry plateaus of their native Spain, and they adapted themselves to its rigors remarkably well.

The golden-armored leader sent scouting parties in several directions. He himself rode all the way into what is now Kansas, lured by the tales told him by captured Indians. One by one the groups returned with word of failure; no great cities were to be found, and no treasure. Yet, though the fact meant little to them at the time, this ill-fated expedition bent on plunder was doing a tremendous service for future generations by exploring and roughly charting the American desert. For the first time the world was learning what existed in this far corner of the new continent.

One of Coronado's captains, Melchior Diaz, led a group across the heat-seared, cactus-dotted plain of Arizona, crossed the Colorado River and penetrated into what is now the desert country of Southern California. There the battle-scarred veteran died in a strange accident. A lance which he had thrown at his dog in a fit of anger stuck in the ground and Diaz, unable to stop his horse in time, was fatally impaled on its shaft. He became the first white man to perish on the California desert.

Another party discovered one of the world's most spectacular natural wonders, the Grand Canyon of the Colorado. Striking north across the sandy desert of Arizona, the Spanish horsemen climbed into the higher rocky region where patches of forest alternate with sterile, brilliant-hued desert. Suddenly they found themselves on the rim of a canyon, so immense and startling in its coloring and depth that they stared in amazement.

Four centuries have passed since these first explorers stood on the canyon rim in the wilderness. Yet the scenic view they beheld is exactly the same today, and strikes the thousands of tourists who come by automobile and train with the same overpowering feeling of awe.

Before them is a jagged gash in the earth, so wide and deep that at first the eye cannot grasp its true dimensions.

The far side lies miles to the north. Far, far below the rim, barely visible between the jagged hills which rise from the canyon floor, is a tiny stream, seemingly only a few inches wide. Those who make the adventurous trip down the canyon trail on mules, however, find that this is the broad and turbulent Colorado River, churning dozens of miles through the canyon in a series of rapids.

From hour to hour, even minute to minute, the coloring on the rocky walls and along the rugged depths of the canyon changes. Deep red blends with purple shadows, a distant rock face gleams orange and gray, then shafts of sunlight penetrate the sheltered depths of a side canyon, followed perhaps by flashes of lightning as a thunderstorm moves through the gorge far below. Here is the most breathtaking example of erosion to be found anywhere in the world.

The first white men spent two years on the American desert, gathering intangible riches of this sort. But they went back to Mexico City bitterly disappointed because they wanted gold and had found none. The dream of the Seven Cities of Gold had dissolved into a nightmare. Yet the expedition had done something far greater—it had explored a huge area of southwestern America and made the white man's imprint on the ancient desert for the first time.

For half a century after Coronado's adventure the Spaniards ignored the desert. Its rigors and emptiness offered no attractions sufficiently strong to coax them north from the comforts of Mexico City and the wealth of the

Mexican mines. To them it was only a remote wasteland which had proved a disappointment. Life on the desert droned on as it had for centuries, centered in the Indian communities scattered at wide intervals. Coronado's army became just a memory for the old men of the pueblos to talk about as they sat in the sun.

Then in 1598 the leaders of New Spain decided that the vast desert spaces to their north should be colonized. Thousands of miles away, back in the old world, Spain had suffered a disastrous defeat when the English destroyed her mighty Spanish Armada. This led to re-examination of Spain's colonial position in the world. Perhaps the desert was worth occupying, after all. Also, the Spanish priests were anxious to convert the Indians to Christianity.

Chosen as leader of the new expedition was a haughty, fearless and ruthless commander named Juan de Oñate. His army, looking much like Coronado's nearly sixty years earlier, marched north. It reached the Rio Grande about twenty-five miles below what is now El Paso, Texas.

"I claim this land in the name of Spain," Oñate announced. "I name it New Mexico."

He told the Indians that they were now under the protection of the Spanish crown and must become Christians. This failed to arouse their enthusiasm, since they did not want protection and were content with their own religion.

The priests who accompanied the army set about their missionary work. They were brave, dedicated men who walked or rode mules hundreds of miles across the desert from one Indian community to another. The natives called the priests "wetheads" because they sprinkled water on the heads of those they baptized.

From the Rio Grande, Oñate marched his army westward. They reached Acoma, the sky city perched high on its mesa, and received its grudging surrender. Shortly after Oñate's main force had marched on, another detachment of Spaniards came to Acoma.

Led by Juan de Zaldivar, they climbed the narrow trail up the cliffside, thinking they were to be given gifts and food in token of the Indians' loyalty. Instead, they were attacked by the Acomans. Zaldivar was killed by a blow from a club.

News of the ambush was rushed to Oñate, and he sent Vicente de Zaldivar, brother of the slain captain, with seventy men to punish Acoma. These Spaniards faced a hazardous task against several hundred Indians barricaded 350 feet in the sky. But their zeal and bravery was tremendous.

The battle raged for three days. The mesa was a shambles of bodies, arrows and swords as the Spanish dragged their single cannon up the sheer walls and stormed the fortress. Acoma paid a high price for its treachery—500 of its people dead.

Spanish rule over the American desert had been preserved. If Acoma had beaten the Spaniards, the other conquered pueblos would have revolted. The white man might have been driven completely from the region, leaving it to be sparsely occupied only by the primitive native tribes which had existed there for hundreds of years without doing anything to develop it.

Oñate roamed far and wide across the southwestern desert, reinforcing the Spanish hold on the area. Visitors to a certain towering white sandstone bluff on the western edge of New Mexico, called Inscription Rock, can still see his autograph carved into the stone. Three centuries of sun, wind and rain have failed to wipe out the words, apparently carved with the point of his sword while returning from his journey following the Colorado River all the way south to its mouth at the Gulf of California. Written in Spanish, they read:

"Passed by here the Commander Don Juan de Oñate from the discovery of the sea of the South on the 16th of April, 1605."

Known today as El Morro National Monument, this rock mass stands as a unique history book, a picturesque reminder that it was the Spaniards who first opened thousands of miles of the United States to the white man. Other desert pioneers, following Oñate's example, cut their names in this stone autograph album. At its foot is the natural basin of water which made it the stopping place for caravans. Close study of it discloses the signatures of other Spanish commanders, U. S. Army officers who came that way more than 200 years later seeking good emigrant trails to the west and, more recently, those

of pioneers who drove wagon trains and cattle herds to California.

Even at its height, however, the Spanish occupation of the desert was a thin one, with only a few thousand white men living in the tens of thousands of square miles which make up this parched, sprawling region. Yet the Spanish language, hundreds of Spanish place names and many mission churches—integral parts of desert life today—attest to the strength of Spanish influence. The Spaniards brought cattle and sheep, and introduced the Indians to the wonders of the wheel and metals.

Father Junipero Serra founded a line of missions from San Diego to San Francisco Bay. From these, towns were to grow and Spanish rule was established along the California coast. But there were no white men from the pueblos of Arizona westward across the desert. Many miles separated the settlements of California and those of Spanish New Mexico.

Far across the vast continent were the newly created United States. The Americans were busy developing their new country and carving homesteads out of the wilderness east of the Mississippi River. They gave little heed to the communities lying far to the west.

By 1825, however, a few adventurous Americans were exploring these empty spaces, mostly in search of furs. A daring journey of this kind across the western desert became the first direct link by land between the white men of the Atlantic coast and those of California.

His fellow mountain men called him Diah Smith, this tall, clean-shaven and adventurous trapper, but his full name was Jedediah Strong Smith. He was of that restless breed of pioneer men and hardly had he turned twenty-one than he started west from his native village in upstate New York. He arrived in the frontier town of St. Louis carrying his rifle and his Bible, then headed up the Missouri River with a party of trappers. Through the mountains and forests of the Northwest, lands never before visited by white men, they hunted beaver and other animals whose pelts were in demand.

On a hot August day in 1826, at the age of twenty-seven, Jedediah Smith started from the Great Salt Lake, in what is now Utah, upon an adventure of historic note. Still in pursuit of furs, not fame, he and his hunting party first crossed the great American desert from the east, blazing a trail that in later years would bring many thousands of Americans westward.

The cavalcade that rode south from the Great Salt Lake consisted of eighteen men and fifty horses. Saddle bags were loaded with American goods to be traded to the Indians—knives, mirrors, buttons, ribbons, iron arrow points, kettles, tobacco.

They also carried 700 pounds of dried buffalo meat, having no idea of how much game they would be able to shoot in the unknown lands to the southwest. Even this foresight was not enough; soon they rode out onto the parched and barren desert where no game was to be found. After a few weeks their hunger became a gnawing, torturing thing. The party worked its way into the mountains of southern Utah along the Sevier River, across the divide and down into the rocky canyons of the Virgin River. They were fairly into the desert. Grass for the horses grew more and more sparse. One by one the thin, weary animals faltered, unable to carry loads further, or even to keep up with the party. Out of mercy Smith and his men had to shoot the horses, rather than leave them to perish.

Jedediah Smith had no maps to guide him. All he knew was the vague fact that far to the west—nobody knew how far—were Spanish settlements on the Pacific coast. What lay between was veiled in mystery. No white men had come this way before.

Eventually, after crossing a large river which we know as the Colorado, the party came upon the fertile valley of the Mojaves. Diah Smith was generous in distributing the shining trinkets from the saddle bags. Fascinated, the Indians received the white men kindly. Supplied with fresh horses and with two Indians as guides, Smith and his men pushed on, and entered the worst desert of all they had seen. This was the great Mojave.

Later, describing the desert crossing, Jedediah Smith wrote, "I traveled a west course fifteen days over a country of complete barrens, generally traveling from morning to night without water. I crossed a salt plain about twenty miles long and eight wide; on the surface was a crust of beautiful white salt, quite thin. Under this surface there is a layer of salt from ½ to 1½ inches in depth; between this and the upper layer is about four inches of yellowish sand."

This salt plain is Soda Lake, a dry lake bed into which the dry Mojave River flows. This sounds impossible, but it is quite true. Most of the time the Mojave is an underground river as it flows east across the desert from the San Bernardino mountains. Although there is moisture several feet under the surface, the ground is a sandy valley without a trickle of water showing for many miles.

Smith and his men followed the Mojave valley. Their buckskin clothes were in tatters. Their food was low, they struggled to find water holes, their horses were dying. Although it was November, the midday heat was so overpowering that the men suffered intensely.

One day, looking at the dragging, exhausted procession, Jedediah Smith called a halt. He had an idea. "If we dig holes in the desert sand, maybe we can find moisture and get relief from the heat," he said.

The men set to work, scooping up sand and gravel until they had small pits three or four feet deep. The sand was wet! Gratefully they crawled into the holes and packed the cool, moist sand around their bodies.

Thus revived, the party pushed ahead. Before them rose a range of mountains covered with forests, their highest peaks capped with snow. At last the goal was in sight. As the men neared the mountains, the Mojave River showed water above the ground.

From a peak Jedediah Smith looked to the west and saw

a glorious sight. Spread out for more than fifty miles between him and the blue Pacific Ocean were trees, grass,
meandering streams along which flocks of cattle grazed:
things which the exhausted desert travelers had almost
forgotten existed. They drank in the view greedily, as if
they could never get enough of it.

Smith led the party down onto the plain and to the
Spanish mission at San Gabriel. The priests received them
gladly, fed them, provided cloth for new clothing and
listened in amazement to the story of their adventures.

The trail across the American continent had been
opened. Men had come the whole width of the continent
and linked the bustling young United States with the
leisurely old world civilization of the Spanish colonies in
California. It was the first trickle of a mighty flood to
follow.

In a narrow wooded valley far back in the lofty Sierras,
through which the American River flowed toward Sutter's
fort at Sacramento, a sawmill was being built. The plan
was to bring trees from the surrounding hills, cut them
and float the logs down the river fifty miles to the fort.

James Marshall, a master carpenter, was in charge of the
job. Halfway through the construction he found that the
mill's tailrace had been dug improperly so that the mill-
wheel would not turn. A blast of dynamite was necessary
to deepen the channel.

On the morning of January 24, 1848, Marshall walked
along the tailrace to see how much of the debris the river

had carried away overnight. Something shining on a ledge a few inches under water caught his eye . . . a kind of rock he had never seen before.

Marshall fished it out. It glittered, but was too heavy to be mica. He struck it with another stone. Instead of breaking off, the yellow stuff merely bent.

Excitedly, Marshall ran back to where the others were working and exclaimed, "Boys, I believe I have found a gold mine!"

He was right. Gold had been discovered in California. From this chance find the magic cry of "Gold!" swept across the continent and the rush of 1849 began. Thousands of adventurers headed across America in wagon trains, intent on growing wealthy in this magic land where gold lay waiting to be picked up.

To reach California they had to cross the desert. The vast barren lands—shimmering hot, almost waterless and treacherous with unknown perils—were a dreaded barrier in the path to riches.

5 Disaster in Death Valley

From a mile-high rocky pinnacle called Dante's View, in the barren Black Mountains of the eastern California desert, a visitor sees a spectacular sight.

Straight down is the lowest point in the United States, a salt-encrusted pond named Badwater, 282 feet below sea level. Without taking a step, merely by lifting his eyes skyward, he looks upon the snow-capped Sierra Nevadas. There stands Mount Whitney, rising 14,495 feet, the highest point in the country outside Alaska.

Before him is spread Death Valley.

The valley is a place of unpleasant superlatives—the hottest, driest, loneliest and most desolate spot in the western hemisphere. All the dreary and disagreeable things that come into people's minds when they think of the desert are embodied here. Not a blade of grass grows in the heart of Death Valley; for many square miles the flat earth stretching between high mountain walls is mottled gray and white, without a speck of vegetation. In summer the temperature in the shade rises to a suffocating 134 degrees.

On Christmas Eve, 1849, a straggling line of covered wagons bumped along a dry creek bed into this valley through a gap in the Funeral Mountains from the east. White men saw the valley that came to be known as Death Valley for the first time that night and they hated what they saw. They had stumbled through the mountains by accident on their way across the uncharted desert to the California gold fields. They were lost and starving. Their hungry oxen barely could drag the wagons. For people exhausted and ill-equipped there was no place in America so forbidding, so devoid of life-giving substances and so difficult to escape.

The story of the Death Valley party is one of the sagas of the American desert . . . a blend of tragedy, suffering, faith and heroic rescue. Twenty-seven wagons creaked into the valley, carrying approximately a hundred people. Only one of those wagons was ever to leave that deadly vale.

A weather-beaten young man in buckskin rode up to a line of covered wagons dozing in the autumn sunshine of

Utah, near the Mormon settlement of Salt Lake City. From the rear of a wagon stepped a woman who peered at the approaching stranger. A look of surprised recognition spread across her face.

"Lewis!" she exclaimed. "Lewis Manly! Where in the world have you come from?"

"Mrs. Bennett!" he replied, almost at the same instant. "I've been looking for you and Asabel all the way from Wisconsin."

They seized each other by the hand and talked excitedly about the remarkable coincidence of meeting so many hundreds of miles from their home village. When Asabel Bennett returned to camp there was another joyous reunion. The men agreed that Lewis Manly should join the expedition across the desert to California as scout and hunter, little dreaming that he would one day save them from a tragic death.

The wagons had been gathering for weeks, many small parties of emigrants having joined forces for the journey. Because it was already autumn, and they knew about the tragedy that had beset the Donner wagon party in the winter snows of the Sierra, this train had decided to take the longer and warmer, but little known southern route. Los Angeles was their goal.

The southerly desert route would take them hundreds of miles out of the way and had never been used by a wagon train before. A Mormon guide who knew the route was hired, and the train was formally organized. The members chose a prophetic name for their expedition—

the Sand Walking Company.

Late in October the long caravan departed. There were 107 covered wagons, about 500 horses and cattle and approximately as many people. Many families carried everything they owned in their wagons to start life afresh in California.

Things went well for a few days. Then somebody passed around a map he had acquired in Salt Lake City which showed a short cut. According to this authentic-looking chart, hundreds of miles could be saved if the wagons left the southwesterly Los Angeles trail in southern Utah and headed straight west.

Quickly the short cut became the dominant item of discussion. Should the wagons follow it or not? The Mormon guide said he did not believe the map and doubted whether any white man had ever taken such a route.

"You all know that I was hired to go by way of Los Angeles," he said. "But if all of you wish to take the short cut I will go also. However, if even one wagon decides to go by the original route, I shall feel duty bound by my promise to go with that lone wagon."

When the procession reached the place where the short cut veered off from the main route, there were tense moments. As each wagon came to the turnoff, the driver either held his oxen straight ahead or swung them to the right. When Asabel Bennett's turn came, he took the short cut, as the majority of wagons had done.

Three days along the cutoff, trouble began. When the wagons reached the summit of a mountain range there seemed no way down the other side. Many of the drivers turned their wagons around and hurried back to rejoin the Los Angeles party. By the time a passage was found, only twenty-seven wagons remained. These were to form the tragic Death Valley party.

The route grew more desolate. Water holes were scarce and hard to find, and the soil was sandy with only a sprinkling of dry leafless shrubs. The oxen became gaunt and weak. On many nights the wagons were drawn up in a dry camp, with no water for the stock or for the humans —only what had been hauled along in containers from the last spring.

By this time the alluring map had been proven worthless. There was no track of any kind across the dreary miles. As Christmas drew near the party was crawling across the most utterly desolate plain it had yet encountered. Reaching the bleak and jagged row of mountains toward which they had been moving for days, the high wheels of the wagons bumped past a projecting point of rock and out onto level ground.

As they looked around, the emigrants saw nothing to give them hope. They were in a long valley running north and south, about 150 miles long and twenty miles across, with mountain barriers in fantastic jumbles of naked rock on the east and west. The region lies just west of the present-day dividing line between California and Nevada.

They had entered Death Valley.

The valley slopes downward from its high point in the north, where Death Valley Scotty's remarkable castle now stands. At the place where the wagon train lumbered out

of a dry creek wash, the valley floor is exactly at sea level. Winds frequently whip through the area, blowing billows of sand and grit. This was dead land into which the struggling gold-seekers blundered.

Having shown them scant favor for weeks, fortune smiled momentarily upon the thirsty travelers as they entered Death Valley. Their course out of the canyon brought them to the best water for miles around. This tiny stream later became known as Furnace Creek, not because of its heat but because miners built a small smelting furnace there. Visitors to the valley can still see it trickling through Furnace Creek Ranch. The emigrants refreshed themselves with the welcome moisture, but every day they lingered their remaining supplies of food dwindled. They must keep moving. Once more votes were taken around the campfires and decisions made.

The Jayhawkers, a group of thirty young men, decided to strike off to the northwest, but soon discovered that they could not get their wagons out of the valley in that direction. They killed their oxen, burned their wagons and dried the ox meat in the flames. Dividing their food and water supplies evenly, they agreed that from that moment on it was every man for himself. They set out afoot in straggling disorder, each man fighting for life along the route which looked best to him. Many of the Jayhawkers eventually reached the coast and safety, while the bodies of the others were left on the desert where they fell.

The Bennett and Arcane families, with whom Lewis

Manly was traveling, made a different decision. Their plan was to head southward down the valley, then cut across to the west side and seek an opening in the Panamint Mountains there. Near Badwater they turned their wagons westward. To their surprise they encountered ponds of water on the otherwise arid valley floor.

Lewis Manly took a stick and waded in to see whether the footing was too soft to support the wagons. Striking the bottom, he found it to be as solid as rock. From a projecting point he broke off a chunk, brushed away the dirt and found the material to be white. He put a little of it in his mouth. Sure enough. Salt!

The bed of the valley in this area is solid rock salt, partially covered with a thin layer of windblown dirt. This explains why nothing will grow there. Decades later investigators drilled through the massive salt block and found it to be more than a thousand feet thick. It was created by the evaporation of the waters of a prehistoric lake which once filled the valley. Visitors to Death Valley today can break off chunks of salt from the edge of the undrinkable seepage pond at Badwater, exactly as Lewis Manly did a century ago.

That night everyone in the Bennett-Arcane party gathered beside one of the wagons to reach a decision. Passage through the mountains ahead with their wagons seemed impossible. What lay beyond the ominous peaks ahead, nobody knew. Death Valley is a trough, walled by stark, rock outcrops and surrounded by desert in all directions. Turning back was not feasible. There was no relief for hundreds of miles to the rear in the uninhabited wastes they had just crossed.

Finally Asabel Bennett said, "I propose that we select two of our youngest, strongest men and ask them to take some food and go ahead to try to seek a settlement. We will wait at the spring for their return. It will surely not take them more than ten days for the trip."

The rest of the party agreed. The rescue team was to bring back information about the route ahead, and emergency food supplies. Lewis Manly and John Rogers, a husky young man from Tennessee, were chosen for the mission upon whose fortunes and safe return the lives of all depended.

Left behind in the camp were fifteen persons, four of them boys and girls, the youngest only two years old.

Manly and Rogers, with scant provisions from the pitifully small supply, climbed to the top of the Panamints and looked westward. Instead of finding signs of life and vegetation, as they had hoped, they saw only a parched desert plain stretching interminably westward, broken by clusters of low mountains as dry and treeless as the plain itself. To reach relief, they must cross this forbidding wasteland.

Day after day they trudged across the rocky sands. They perspired so heavily that their bodies were wrung almost dry. Often they stopped to dig for moisture in likely-looking places, only to find more sand at the bottom of the holes. They obtained slight relief from the clogging dryness in their mouths by chewing bullets. This induced a slight

flow of saliva. Growing hungry, they tried to eat the meat they carried in their knapsacks, but their mouths were so dry they could not swallow it.

Manly wrote later, "We traveled along for hours, never speaking, for we found it much better for our thirst to keep our mouths closed as much as possible, and prevent evaporation. The dry air of that region took up water as a sponge does. Those who have never felt the extreme of thirst cannot imagine the distress, the despair it brings. I can find no words, no way, to express it so others can understand."

Along their route they found the body of a Jawhawker. He had perished of thirst and famine. Later they came across the body of a second man, who had crawled four miles on his hands and knees in a vain effort to reach water. The desert was taking its toll.

Early one cold January morning Manly and Rogers discovered a small sheet of ice in the shadows, no thicker than a window pane. Such ice forms occasionally during midwinter nights in higher desert altitudes. Greedily each man thrust a piece of ice in his mouth. The feel of cold water trickling down their throats was sublime. There was enough ice to fill a quart kettle, and when they had melted it they were able to eat some meat. Luck was with them. Had they come along a few hours later, when the sun was burning high, the ice would have been melted and the water absorbed in the sand.

Thus revived, they pushed ahead. Slowly signs of civilization grew more frequent—a test shaft made by miners, two horses running loose, a house in park-like surroundings and finally, people.

"Such a scene of abundance and rich plenty and comfort bursting thus upon our eyes, which for months had seen only the desolation and sadness of the desert, was like getting a glimpse of Paradise, and tears of joy ran down our faces," Manly said later.

He and Rogers had come out into the San Fernando Valley at Mission San Fernando, about thirty miles northwest of the pueblo of Los Angeles. The Spanish-speaking Californians of the coastal region had difficulty at first in comprehending the story Manly and Rogers told. They regarded the desert on their eastern doorstep as a place of mystery and hardship, onto which they never ventured.

Being young and sturdy, the two messengers revived quickly from their ordeal and were anxious to start the return trip. They bought supplies of food and loaded them on three horses and a mule. Thoughts of those awaiting their return weighed heavily upon them. They dreaded facing the desert hardships again, but already they had been gone much longer than anyone had anticipated. How many of their friends were still alive?

The heat and dryness again began to take their toll. The horses drooped so badly that the men dismounted and walked. Only the mule remained perky and strong. All the load was shifted to her back.

Climbing a rocky canyon through the treeless range of mountains separating them from Death Valley, Manly and Rogers came to an imposing rock face. The mule scrambled to the top, but the horses could not make it. They had to be abandoned.

As they came down the eastern slope of the Panamints they found the body of Captain Culverwell, who had struck out for himself and died on the trail.

How many more had done the same? Would anyone be left alive at the spring? Manly and Rogers speculated on these questions.

About noon they saw covered wagons ahead. When they had left four weeks before, there had been seven wagons. Now there were only four. Not a person to be seen. Fear-ing that the Indians had attacked the party and might still be lying in ambush, Manly and Rogers crept forward. A hundred yards from the wagons they still could see no signs of life.

Manly raised his Colt rifle and fired a shot into the air. For a moment nothing happened. Then a gaunt bearded man crawled out from under one of the wagons and looked around in bewilderment. It was Bennett.

Seeing the men, he threw his arms high over his head and shouted, "The boys have come! The boys have come!"

Others emerged from the shade of the wagons and rushed toward the rescuers they had thought would never arrive. Bennett and Arcane embraced the pair with all their strength. Mrs. Bennett fell to her knees and clung to Manly ferociously, her emaciated body wracked with sobs.

"Good boys! O, you have saved us all! God bless you forever!" she exclaimed through her tears.

When the excitement died down, Manly and Rogers broke the news that the entire party must walk 250 miles through desert mountains and plains before they could reach safety. The rescuers in turn learned that the other three wagons were gone because the unattached men in the party had given up hope of rescue and had struck out for themselves.

There was no time to waste. The trip out must be started quickly while the food supplies remained.

Everything the emigrants had brought along for their new homes must be abandoned. They could take nothing but the clothes they were wearing, a few cooking utensils and food. Two water kegs were strapped across the back of an ox.

Mrs. Arcane had brought along some fine clothes to wear when she reached California. "If I can't take anything but what I can wear, then I shall wear my very best clothes," she announced. She donned her gay hat and trimmed it with extra ribbons which streamed behind as she walked across the desolate, sand-blown plains. The children, too, were dressed in their finest, as though they were going to Sunday School.

It was early February when the procession left the spring and started westward again.

At the top of the mountains the travelers halted and looked back into the grim regions which had brought them so much suffering. The men took off their hats and someone said, "Goodbye, Death Valley!" Thus the white men who first knew its torments gave the region its name.

But if they were out of Death Valley at last, their troubles were not yet over. Days of thirst and misery were to follow. But every step brought the party nearer to safety. At last they reached the mountains, and a creek in which they could drink their fill and wash. Almost unbelieving, the emigrants realized that they were safe.

On March 7, 1850, they came to the first house on the coastal side of the desert, set in a meadow and shaded by oak trees. Four months and three days had passed since the Sand Walking Company had taken the fatal short cut. Thirteen of the group had died along the way and the others had escaped by the narrowest of margins, thanks to their determination, the skill of their rescuers and their faith.

Death Valley today is a national monument covering 3,000 square miles of desert and mountains. On a high point where Furnace Creek wash emerges onto the valley floor stands a luxury resort hotel, the Furnace Creek Inn. A mile away is Furnace Creek Ranch, on the site where the emigrants camped. Dozens of cabins accomodate visitors during the winter months. Nearby is a large trailer park. Wells provide ample water, even for a swimming pool, and trucks bring in provisions over paved roads.

Tourists speed into Death Valley in air-conditioned automobiles along the same route the emigrants drove their ox teams, covering as many miles in a single hour as the pioneers did in three days.

Most of Death Valley is exactly as the Sand Walkers found it, however, except for a few roads. A motorist driving south from Furnace Creek travels some seventy miles before he sees another house. If he looks away from the ribbon of black asphalt across the salt flats toward the mountains, it is easy to imagine himself in that pioneer party.

Freed of worries about food and water, the visitor to Death Valley finds much beauty. The colors of the mountains change a dozen times a day as the sun strikes the rocks from different angles, and the drab flatness of the valley untouched by vegetation is a unique sight. The rangers assigned to the monument tell fascinating stories of the region's geology, animal and plant life, and the history of gold, silver and borax mining there. In Salt Creek, which flows only a mile in the upper valley before being swallowed by the sand, there are salt water sardines less than an inch long. Apparently they are descendants of the fish which once lived in the valley's prehistoric lake.

The spring where the emigrant party camped is marked on today's maps as Bennett's Well. It can be reached by an unpaved road.

Ever since the story of the Death Valley party became known, desert men have discussed what the travelers should have done. Their great mistake, of course, was taking the cutoff. But even in their plight while waiting at Bennett's Well, they could have helped themselves if they had known what to do. Around this water hole there is vegetation, including mesquite trees. As the Indians have known for hundreds of years, the pods of the mesquite can be mashed into tasty and nourishing meal. Had the men taken the oxen into the Panamints, they could have found better water and possibly game to shoot.

As for the route out, the trail taken by those emigrants who stayed with their Mormon guide on the planned course was the sensible one. All of them got through safely.

It is easy for men of later times, with the knowledge acquired by generations of pioneers, to say what the Death Valley party did wrong. Their migration was marred by poor planning, mistakes, bad luck and above all, by failure to realize the vastness of the desert. Yet few stories in the opening of the West can match theirs for bravery and undaunted determination to survive.

6 The U. S. Army Camel Corps

A desert campfire on a moonlight night is a time for spinning tales. The eerie white glow spreads across the empty lands and the campers draw close around the low-burning fire pungent with mesquite branches. City life seems remote . . . almost another world from this congenial circle half-hidden in the flickering light.

It is at such moments that old desert men tell the legend of the white camel. This ghostly animal, with eyes red as rubies, is said to roam the American desert carrying the skeleton of a man lashed across his back.

The skeleton is that of a Turkish camel driver who came to the western desert many years ago from his ancient land. As he lay dying he told those at his bedside, "Tie me across the back of my camel and turn him loose. Let him roam wherever he will, so that when the moonlight is bright enough, men can see him and remember me."

Ever since, the camel with its ghostly burden has stalked across the desert. When the moon is low campers may see the shadowy creature marching in lonely grandeur across the horizon.

The legend of the white camel is not all imagination. Once Turkish camels really did roam the arid lands of the American desert, abandoned and unwanted, and their drivers were familiar figures in the mining camps. They were the remnants of the U. S. Army Camel Corps, a strange episode in American military history, and in the history of the desert.

The adventures of the Camel Corps began in a muddy corral outside the old town of San Antonio, Texas, one June evening shortly before the War Between the States. Leaning on the bars of the corral, a young man of nineteen saw a picturesque sight—twenty-five camels plodding single file through the mud. Huge, waddling beasts they were, signaling their approach with the jingle of bells hanging from their necks.

"What ungainly animals!" May Stacey exclaimed to his friend, Ham Porter.

"Yes, and how they smell!" Ham held his nose in mock disgust. "I wonder if we'll be used to that odor by the time we get these camels to California."

Stacey straightened up suddenly and shouted, "Look out! The horses are going crazy."

Indeed, they were. The horses and mules were terrified by the sight and smell of the weird, humped animals. They dashed wildly around the corral, heads erect, snorting in alarm. Nothing like this had ever been seen in western America.

The camels, under the close watch of their Turkish and Greek drivers, remained undisturbed by the hubbub. They chewed their cuds with a deliberate motion of their loose, pouting lips. Horses were nothing new in their lives. They had seen many back in their native countries of the Middle East. But the swift, high-strung Texas horses could not comprehend these shaggy beasts. Comanche arrows whirring past their heads as they raced across the prairies had never disturbed them so much.

After a few days, however, the horses and mules reluctantly came to tolerate the camels. The truce was an uneasy one, but good enough to permit departure of one of the strangest caravans the U. S. Army had ever conducted.

The War Department had decided to establish a camel corps on the desert as a means of bridging the mammoth gaps between Army posts and the scattering of tiny settlements. The year was 1857, just four years before the first shot was fired at Fort Sumter. The expedition was starting on a 1,500-mile trek through hostile Indian territory and across the sands of the desert to California. Its orders were two-fold: blaze a new emigrant trail across New Mexico and Arizona, and determine how the camels could be put to use in the wastelands of America.

The men who had conceived the camel corps idea were confident. They believed that camels would prove to be exactly the right kind of animals for crossing the American desert with its huge dry distances, because of their ability to go without water and withstand heat. Soon, they thought, these lumbering creatures would be carrying the mail, hauling freight and providing fast transportation for soldiers between the thinly garrisoned frontier forts. Weren't the animals in daily use as riding mounts and beasts of burden around the Pyramids in Egypt?

The California-bound caravan was led by a veteran trailmaker of the American desert, Lieutenant Edward F. Beale. The twenty-five camels in his charge were the choicest animals a military purchasing party had been able to obtain in the Middle East. They already had shown their stamina by surviving a sea voyage from Turkey to Texas.

The men in Beale's party were a rough-and-ready lot. Soldiers, frontiersmen and Mexican ranch hands shared the roster with camel drivers brought from the Middle East. May Stacey, Hampden Porter and Joseph Bell were the sons of Lieutenant Beale's family neighbors back in Chester, Pennsylvania, and were getting their first look at the West. They little guessed the adventures and trials ahead in the parched and barren desert, a land so unlike anything they had known. May Stacey kept a diary, writing by the campfire each night along the trail, and it is to him that we owe much of our knowledge about that journey of nearly five months.

Among the drivers were two particularly colorful young men. One was a youth named Greek George. The other was a teen-age Syrian lad named Hadji Ali. Such a foreign name was too much for the plain-spoken men of the frontier to handle, so he quickly became known as Hi Jolly.

Clamorous confusion marked the departure of the caravan. The camp cooks were up at two-thirty in the morning, getting breakfast for an early start. The oaths of the muleskinners mingled with the high barbaric-sounding calls of the camel drivers and the tinkling of bells. Some of the mules balked at being harnessed. The camels did not like the heavy loads of corn hoisted across their humps, 576 pounds to each animal. They spat in anger at their handlers. They moved so slowly that by the time they had covered the day's march of sixteen miles they were hours behind the mules.

That night May Stacey wrote down his view, which was widely shared in camp, "It is my decided opinion that these camels will prove a failure."

Events proved him wrong, however. A half century later some of those camels were still running wild on the desert. They had adapted themselves to their new surroundings. But their masters had lost interest in them, and the camel experiment had been forgotten in the turmoil of war. The failure was by the men, not the animals. One of the

82

camels, Topsy, lived for another seventy-seven years and ended her long life behind the bars of the Griffith Park zoo in Los Angeles in 1934.

By a strange twist in history, the man who made the camel corps possible indirectly helped bring it to an end. Secretary of War Jefferson Davis was the official who in 1855 talked Congress into appropriating $30,000 for the purchase of camels to be used by the U.S. Army. He knew nothing about camels, but he had fought as an American officer in the Mexican War and knew the huge distances on the southwestern frontier.

Beale and others had built up his enthusiasm for the experiment, and after two years of trying he succeeded in getting the money from Congress. Six years later, however, this same Jefferson Davis had become President of the Confederacy and was leading the South against the North. He, along with everyone else, was too busy to think about camels.

To obtain the beasts of burden for this desert corps of the new world, two American officers had gone to the Middle East. Their plan was to purchase the finest creatures they could obtain on the deserts of Egypt, Syria and Turkey, where camels had been used since ancient times, and bring them to America in a specially-rigged Navy store ship. The *Supply* had been remodelled for its peculiar task before leaving the Brooklyn navy yard.

Quickly Major Henry Wayne and Lieutenant David Porter, the purchasing agents, learned that buying camels had its pitfalls. They bought some of the lighter and faster one-humped creatures, called dromedaries, and also the two-humped variety, known as Bactrian camels, as they sailed the *Supply* to half a dozen ports from Egypt to Turkey.

The first camel had no sooner been brought aboard the ship than it developed the itch. The extent of this misfortune from the camel's standpoint may be appreciated if one recalls that curse of the Arab world, "May you have the camel's itch!" The sailors rubbed and curried the animal, fed it sulphur and twice a day oiled its knee callouses.

There was trouble, too, because one animal was too tall for the sea-going stable. He was seven feet and five inches high and could not stand up straight because his hump bumped the ceiling. Ingenious seamen cut a hole in the deck above so that the top of the beast's hump stuck through.

At last the ship sailed in February, 1856, from Smyrna to the United States. After a rough three months the *Supply* reached the small port of Indianola, Texas, about 120 miles south of Galveston. The camels kicked and reared in excitement when they stepped onto firm ground again. It was some months later when the caravan finally headed west.

The Americans found handling camels a very different proposition than coaxing mules. Some climbed aboard the beasts to ride but soon slid down, deathly seasick. The rolling, pitching motion on the top deck of a camel is as bad as the cavorting of a small sailboat in a choppy sea.

Gradually the camels settled to their task and made better time. Some days the straggling procession advanced as much as thirty miles in its progress from the rolling plains into mountainous country. Lieutenant Beale wrote back enthusiastic reports to the Secretary of War about his camels' behavior. He was especially pleased because as they entered the dry regions the camels ate the greasewood shrub of their own accord, preferring this dry unappetizing growth to the grass. A good sign, he thought, because in some parts of the desert there is far more greasewood than edible grass.

Although they had no metal shoes, the camels also pleased their masters with their ability to walk through the sharp, flinty gravel that covered parts of the desert trail. The camel has no shuffle to its gait, but lifts each foot perpendicularly and puts it down flat without sliding, as most four-footed animals do.

Lieutenant Beale wrote to the Secretary, "It gives me great pleasure to report the entire success of the expedition with the camels so far . . . although we have used the camels every day with heavy packs we have far fewer sore backs and disabled ones than would have been the case traveling with pack mules."

May Stacey and his companions from the East were worrying much more about Indians by this time than about the camels. They had entered Comanche country. Guards were posted every night to warn against a surprise attack. There was genuine reason for worry. The graves of earlier users of the trail who had been attacked by Indians could be seen at several of the watering places where overnight halts were made.

Week followed week as the expedition moved slowly westward through southern Texas, across the Rio Grande and into southeastern New Mexico. It was August. The weather was scorching and the ground was changing from grasslands to semi-desert terrain. Watering places were rare. At times the expedition had to exist from the supply of water the camels hauled on their backs in old wooden barrels. Lieutenant Beale made jubilant note of the fact that in one stretch the camels went twenty-six hours without a drop of water—an experience, he said, which would have driven the mules wild.

As it started north in central New Mexico toward the settlement of Albuquerque the expedition came to the feared Deadman's Journey, or *Jornada del Muerto.* This is a stretch of ninety miles through the desert without water, the most hated part of the old Spanish trail from the settlements around Santa Fe down to Mexico. Many were the tales on the southwestern frontier about its miseries. The terrain was heavy sand in places, turning into a plain of gama grass and cactus plants. Off to the west was the big bend of the Rio Grande and to the east rose the sharply etched San Andreas mountains. Hundreds of cattle had perished here from thirst during the decades that the Spanish and Mexicans had used the trail. Here indeed was a test for the camels.

Beale decided to travel at night by moonlight because

86

of the intense heat, a practice still followed by many of those who cross the desert in midsummer. Luck was with the party. Hardly had they entered the *Jornada* than that rare treat, a rain, began falling. A piece of good fortune! Rain fell intermittently all four days of the crossing. What had been one of the most feared parts of the California trip passed more easily than anyone could have hoped.

These summer rains occur at times in parts of the American desert, usually in the form of short, intense thunderstorms. The accumulated dryness of centuries has left the desert soil so thirsty, however, that the rain is quickly absorbed, leaving no trace of moisture apparent a few hours after the downpour ceases. Such scattered rains are a boon to the desert traveler, but have no lasting effect upon the intensely dry ground.

The only settlements seen by the camel caravan for hundreds of miles were the occasional clusters of mud huts, mostly inhabited by Mexicans. These isolated desert dwellers kept mistaking the expedition for a traveling show, about whose wonders they had heard. One of the wagons had been painted a bright red, adding to the impression, which for fun Lieutenant Beale sometimes pretended was true.

When the camel caravan reached the village of Albuquerque it had been on the trail for six weeks. Here it took on supplies for sixty days, knowing that the hardest part of its desert journey lay ahead. A hundred sheep, to be slaughtered en route for fresh meat as a supplement to the ration of hard bread and salt bacon commonly called "Old Ned," were acquired.

At last, after four months, the camel corps approached the Colorado, the chief river of the southwestern desert. Across the stream lay California, the expedition's goal. First, however, camels and men must cross the menacing Mojave desert.

Even before this final test, the camels must be moved across the Colorado, and there was no bridge or boat to transport them. Lieutenant Beale was deeply worried because he had been told the animals could not swim. The Colorado was wide and swift.

Hi Jolly and Greek George pushed the largest and strongest camel into the water, and to the surprise of all the great ungainly animal began to swim clumsily. Beale had the camels tied together in gangs of five, and all swam boldly to the California shore. A dozen of the horses and mules floundered and drowned.

The crossing of the Mojave desert was dry, dreary and exhausting, but with the goal in sight at last the party felt a rising surge of excitement. Just before the Cajon pass, Lieutenant Beale ordered most of the caravan to strike westward to Fort Tejon in the mountains that lie between Los Angeles and Bakersfield. This was to be the camels' home for the present.

The urge to show off his prizes to the settlers of the little pueblo of Los Angeles was too much to resist, how-

ever. The camels were driven through the pass and down into the coastal area.

Outside the pueblo of four thousand inhabitants, the caravan halted long enough for Hi Jolly to change into his native costume of baggy trousers, turban and jacket, ornamented by bells. Tinkling bells also hung on the harness of his camel, Tuili. Riding high in the swaying saddle, Hi Jolly led the procession into the central plaza. The Angelenos had never seen, or even dreamed, anything like this scene out of the Arabian Nights. Their horses reared, dozens of dogs barked and the crowd became so thick that the camels had to be placed in a corral to protect men and beast alike.

For two days the visitors turned life in Los Angeles upside down. Then they were taken the hundred miles north to Fort Tejon and put out to pasture.

The camel corps was in California. It had made the desert crossing safely without the loss of a camel or man. One of the camels had gone ten days without water in a test. But now that they were here, how should the army use the animals?

Nobody quite seemed to know. The camels thrived in two feet of snow at Fort Tejon that winter, occasionally being used to haul supplies from Los Angeles. Once a supply wagon was stuck in the snow so deeply that its team of six mules could not extricate it. Several camels were dispatched to the rescue and soon had it rolling.

Beale made a return trip eastward across the desert and sent such a glowing report to Washington that Secretary of War Floyd tried to get money from Congress for more animals—a thousand camels, in fact—but without success. The Congressmen did not see why they should spend such a large sum for animals to be used in the far-away West. Nevertheless, a few more camels were brought to California.

Beale went back east when the war began and the camels lost their sponsor. Nobody knew what to do with them. They were kept at Fort Tejon for awhile. Later they were moved to Los Angeles, to a corral at what is now Second and Spring Streets, where they became an after-school attraction for boys and girls who loved to ride them when the caretakers were in a cooperative mood. Finally they were moved to an army installation north of San Francisco and sold at auction.

"What am I bid for this splendid animal, this mighty ship of the desert?" The auctioneer's chant was a strange closing dirge for the U. S. Army Camel Corps.

An odd series of adventures and legends grew out of this dispersal of the camels. Some animals were used to carry salt from a Nevada marsh to the Washoe silver mill, a distance of 200 miles. A few found their way into circuses and zoos. The others, unclaimed and unwanted, were turned loose on the desert to fend for themselves.

For years there were reports of the giant beasts stalking their lonely way across the deserts of Southern California and Arizona. Many a prospector who had been searching the hills for gold came into a settlement exclaiming, "The heat is so terrible out there on the desert that it's driving

91

me crazy. Seeing mirages of lakes and palm trees on the sand is bad enough. But now I've seen the mirage of a camel!"

Told that it was a real animal, not a mirage, he would shake his head in amazement and start to show off his bag of ore samples. Gold ore. Now there was something real for a man to see!

In Nevada the animals were much more than a mirage. They became such a public nuisance that the state legislature took action. In 1875 it passed a bill carrying fines up to $100 and jail terms up to thirty days for the owner of any camel caught running loose on a public road.

This law did nothing to curb the wild roamers of the desert. When a camel wandered into a camp of miners or travelers, perhaps with vague memories of his days under human care, his presence caused an uproar among the horses and mules. Men fired their guns at the animal until it padded away into the open spaces, puzzled, no doubt, by the strange ways of men.

Two of the camel drivers brought over from the Middle East also found the American desert to their liking and stayed.

Greek George lived with the Mexicans on the desert fringes so long that he forgot all his Greek and, never learning English, spoke only Spanish. He grew a luxuriant beard, a bit of masculine vanity that saved his life in an Indian fight near Camp Mojave. An arrow struck him but lost most of its force in the matted hair of his beard. Eventually he became an American citizen under the unromantic name of George Allen and grew vegetables near Los Angeles until well into the twentieth century.

Hi Jolly was an even more colorful character. The lure of gold attracted him more than the pungent odor of camels and he became a prospector. Although he roamed the desert with his pick and burro, he never outgrew the liking for the animals he had brought so far from his native land.

He became a scout in Arizona, and his dark, wrinkled figure was a familiar sight in the settlements which developed in that territory during the closing years of the nineteenth century.

Hi Jolly's grizzled countenance was seen around the desert until after the turn of the century. He died in 1903 at Quartzsite, Arizona, a few miles east of the Colorado crossing where the camels swam nearly fifty years earlier. Those are facts. The story of how he died is an odd one; perhaps it is true, perhaps only a desert tale of the romantic kind that the life of Hi Jolly demands.

A prospector came into a saloon at Quartzsite from the back country, telling everyone who would listen about a huge reddish camel he had seen a few miles out of town. One old fellow at the bar showed great interest and pressed the prospector for details. Hi Jolly, for that is who it was, then left the saloon and walked out into the barren land. Three days later he was found dead on the desert, lying with his arms around the neck of the camel. It, too, had perished.

Only a story, perhaps. Be that as it may, the old camel

driver rests forever beneath a pyramid of stones, on which a bronze plaque reads, "The last camp of Hi Jolly." Motorists who pause for a few minutes in the village of Quartzsite can see the grave a few hundred feet north of U.S. Highway 60–70.

Beside Hi Jolly lie the remains of one of those camels he had coaxed and goaded, sung to and cursed on the deserts of the old world and new. When Topsy died in the Los Angeles zoo in 1934, her ashes were taken to Arizona and buried beside those of her master . . . a fitting end to a unique episode in desert history.

7 Sand, Rocks and Wealth

Some men look at the desert and see only parched and treacherous miles of barren land. Others scan the same horizon and say, "Somewhere out there a million dollars is waiting for me. All I have to do is find it."

This is the spirit of that lonely tribe of men, the desert prospectors. For many decades these doughty individualists roamed the American West with their burros, chipping away at rock outcroppings with their picks in the never-waning hope of striking it rich.

Fabulous amounts of gold and silver have been taken from the holes these prospectors dug, to appear later in the cities as fine silverware or gold bracelets, and to make men rich. Ghost towns in the Calicos, the Superstitions, the Panamints, the Funerals and other inhospitable ranges of mountains that criss-cross the desert are today's monuments to these miners.

Turn the car off the transcontinental highway and head up a dirt road into the mountains for a look at one of these ghost towns. Call it Bodie, Greenwater, Harrisburg, Skidoo or any of a hundred other names that once dotted the map of California, Nevada and Arizona. It doesn't matter which one, really, because the stories of all are much alike. But the driver must be careful not to risk breaking the automobile's springs by driving more than five miles an hour up the final stretch of the canyon. Nobody has worried about patching this road in the last forty years. Some abandoned towns can be reached only after a hike of several miles.

Up the canyon the car twists along the way once taken by the stage coaches. High up the slope lies the ghost town. There are a few remnants of stone foundations, chunks of rusty metal and wooden shacks sagging toward collapse.

Not a soul lives in the ruins now, yet for a few years early in the twentieth century 2,000 men and a few dozen women resided here, isolated from the world. The nearest town was more than fifty miles away.

Oftentimes it all began when a prospector lost his burros, a common enough mishap on the desert. These long-eared, sure-footed animals, known also as jackasses or donkeys, not only are splendid pack animals, but are intelligent and wily. When they did not want to work, they merely walked away from camp during the night and dared the prospector to find them.

One old fellow, when asked how long he had been on the desert, replied, "I've been prospectin' around here for thirty years. Twenty of 'em I spent looking fer my burros and the other ten fer gold. Finally I got smart and never let those critters hear me say where I was goin' the next day."

Some of the richest gold and silver strikes were made when prospectors were chasing their burros through the hills. Like Lazy Jim Butler, for example. He was working his way across the desert of western Nevada one day in May, 1900, and had reached a water hole known to the Indians as Tonopah. Jim rolled up in his blanket for the night. The next morning his burros were gone. A windstorm laden with sand was swirling across the desert, and Jim fought his way through it hunting his animals. He found them, safe enough, standing well sheltered behind a ledge. While Jim sat on a rock beside them waiting out the storm he idly chipped at the stones around him.

Later he had the rocks assayed by a man to whom he gave an eighth interest in any resulting profits. The assayer weighed the gold button extracted from the ore, did some rapid calculations and announced, "Jim, this assays at $575 a ton! If the rest of that claim of yours is anything like this, you've hit a fortune."

Which is just what happened to Lazy Jim. So rich was this Tonopah strike that a single shipment of forty-eight tons of ore brought a check for $574,958.39—all because

Jim Butler's burros had enough sense to take shelter from a sandstorm.

The ghost towns seen today had similar beginnings. A prospector picked up some likely-looking ore samples and built a small heap of stones, or monument, to mark his claim in case the rock tested out well. When he reached a camp two or three weeks later he had an assayer run the specimens through his small test furnace and found that they were heavy with gold.

Back to the canyon went the prospector as fast as his burros could carry him. Even so he was only about two jumps ahead of other gold-hungry miners. Word of a strike flashed along the desert's gossip "telegraph" and the rush was on. Hiking, riding horses, driving buckboards as far as they could penetrate into the canyon, or leading their burros, the desert men flocked to the new find.

The discoverer set to digging on his claim, for the law required that he develop the property in order to hold it. Other prospectors tramped up and down the hillsides and valley, trying to figure which way the vein ran so they too could stake a claim. Soon dozens of rock monuments marked the sites of their hopes.

As if by magic a town began to develop. A few tents at first and then, after the arrival of lumber freighted across the desert, a handful of small wooden buildings. The path up the canyon was improved until it formed a dirt road good enough to handle a stagecoach; these rugged vehicles under the whip of an expert driver could penetrate all kinds of unlikely places.

One day an itinerant editor arrived by wagon with a hand press and a case of type, and the town had a newspaper. A general store, an eating house, saloons and other business establishments came into being. Every week the population rose by another hundred or two. The single street rang to the noise of mule teams and stagecoaches, and within a few months the whoomp-whoomp of a mill was heard as it crushed the ore and drew off the precious metal.

For a year or two the mines upon which all this accumulation of people depended poured forth their treasure. Then one day a whisper swept through town, "They say the vein at the Wonder mine is being pinched off. The gold is running out!"

Officials issued denials. "Why, there's even finer gold another fifty feet down. This lode will be greater than the Comstock."

The wise ones knew better because they had seen it happen in other boom towns. The stagecoach began to arrive with empty seats and was overloaded as it departed. The weekly paper appeared carrying the editor's announcement that this was its last edition. The next morning the editor piled his press and type cases aboard a wagon and headed down the grade to a district where the word-of-mouth "telegraph" reported things booming.

The town died almost as fast as it had been born. The desert sun and wind, and sometimes the cloudbursts in the mountains, did their work. Nobody was left to care what happened. Only a few fragments of man's existence remain to mark the site. Yet in its brief and turbulent life the mining town added millions of dollars to the world's wealth, thanks to the prospector who had found a piece of rock and sensed that it was laced with gold.

A few such old prospectors still roam the desert, snooping around the old diggings for overlooked minerals, rarely coming near the main highways. Their modern counterparts do their searching in jeeps, the next best thing to a burro for reaching remote places, but surviving oldtimers sneer at this four-wheeled replacement for the burro.

The ruins of the ghost town can scarcely suggest all the excitement and humor, the tragedy and luck, that once existed here on the desert.

Take the case of Panamint. One of the shrewdest tricks in desert history was played there on a pair of stagecoach robbers who were waiting to seize the camp's shipment of silver.

Rising up the western slope of the Panamint Mountains a short distance from Death Valley is Surprise Canyon. Its rock sides are so close together that a vehicle barely can pass through them. Back in the 1870's men who had reasons to avoid the law used Surprise Canyon as a hideout. They knew that few sheriffs were eager to climb its 6,000-foot rise through all the rocky defiles that were so handy for an ambush.

Two of the outlaws who took refuge there were a pair of stagecoach robbers, John Small and John McDonald. Having halted a Wells, Fargo & Co. coach and seized the money from its box at gunpoint, these two arrived at Surprise Canyon just about the time it was discovered that the walls of the canyon were rich with silver.

Despite their reluctance to have the law snooping around, the badmen of Surprise Canyon had too good a thing to pass up. Small and McDonald staked out a handsome claim. A mining district was formed, claims filed and a boom began. Of all the boom towns, Panamint was perhaps the most difficult to reach. Wagons coming up the grade rolled backward if they were halted without the brakes being set. Going downhill, a freighter had to hitch most of his mules *behind* the wagon to hold it from running away.

Gold or silver bullion to be shipped out was usually in small bars of pure metal, and mining camps turned to the most famous name in western communications, Wells, Fargo & Co., for the precious cargo. With as many as three shotgun messengers on guard, the high-wheeled coaches of Wells, Fargo carried the treasure of the mines in the express box beneath the driver's feet.

Even these dauntless carriers of wealth drew a line, however. They refused to serve Panamint. The profitable percentage that Wells, Fargo collected on the shipments it carried was not enough to overcome their distrust of this town.

Many mining towns have boasted of their lawlessness. Tombstone, Arizona, called itself "the town that is too tough to die." But word of the express company's refusal quickly established Panamint as the terror of the

101

desert. What other camp had such proof of its meanness?

How was the silver to be shipped out? Here were millions in potential riches if only they could reach the market. Transportation costs of the bulky ore shipments by mule team across sixty miles of desert to the nearest town were excessive. Any profitable big-time operation required reduction of the ore on the spot and shipment of the bullion. That was just what Small and McDonald were waiting for.

Two United States Senators from Nevada—William M. Stewart and John P. Jones, the "silver senators"— were partners in some of Nevada's richest mining operations. Willing to take a chance on Panamint, they purchased most of the good claims and set up a stamping mill to reduce the ore.

Small and McDonald watched with anticipation and made their plans. They had sold their mining claim to Senator Stewart, intending all the while to rob the first stage coach headed down the canyon with bullion.

When it came to shipping the silver, however, Senator Stewart outsmarted the robbers. He knew very well what they had in mind. Imagine the surprise of Small and McDonald when the treasure wagon reached the place where they lay in wait. Stewart had melted his silver into five huge balls weighing 450 pounds each! No robber in the world could haul away such mammoth cannonballs. If they stole the entire wagon and tried to drive it sixty miles across the desert to the nearest settlement they quickly would be outraced and caught. If they tried to cut across country the heavy wagon would bog down. They could barely roll one of the balls, let alone lift it.

Panamint's silver rolled safely across the desert the whole time the town's mines were in operation, while the outwitted robbers grumbled at the "injustice."

Few of the prospectors who discovered caches of desert gold and silver ever grew rich. Lazy Jim Butler was an exception. Most sold their claims for a few thousand dollars to the mining operators who followed them. Finding "color" in the rocks meant more to them than the riches the strike might bring.

No more colorful lot of adventurers can be found than these men who chose to risk the desert's heat and thirst, alone for weeks at a time.

John Lamoigne was one of those who spent many years on the desert and dug his living from its soil. Old John, as he was known, was a lone hand, doing much of his traveling in a buckboard drawn by four dusty burros and which held everything he owned. If he stumbled across good ore while roaming the sands, he was ready to start operations immediately.

Most of his life the prospecting paid him sparse dividends. Old John had a private, one-man silver mine in the hills that was his "bank." Careful with his "account," the vein served him adequately. The grief that came into his life arose over too much money, not too little.

Craving more human companionship later in life, Lamoigne built a one-room shack near a water hole known

as Garlic Spring because of its peculiar taste. Travelers
who happened along the seldom-used track nearby stopped
at Old John's place. He would sell them some of his
canned goods if they wished. Eventually he took to grubstaking other prospectors.

Grubstaking is the practice of supplying an ambitious
but impoverished prospector with food and supplies to
sustain him during his treasure search. If he happens to
strike pay dirt, he gives a one-third share of all the mine's
earnings to the grubstaker.

That's how Old John came to have too much money.
Two prospectors whom he had grubstaked as partners
happened to make a paying strike. The money started rolling in, faster than Old John had ever dreamed it could, and
he did not know what to do with it.

Whenever a royalty check came in, he turned it over to
Ma Gibson, a woman he trusted in nearby Piute, with a
request to get it cashed and keep the gold pieces for him.
Ma took the checks into the bank at San Bernardino, and
faithfully cared for John's growing pile of gold. Soon it
grew so large that she worried about the responsibility.
She refused to take care of his money any longer.

Old John thought it over awhile. He did not trust banks.
The only way he could think to spend the money was to
build a house, something so costly it would use up the
money that kept coming in. A monstrosity that became
known as "Old John's Castle" rose at Garlic Spring. The
huge building had round turrets at each corner and a
church-like spire rising from the center of a flat roof. A

wide verandah with ornate railings surrounded the house. There was a music room and library, a crystal chandelier and gold-painted furniture.

But the old prospector was not happy. Other desert prospector friends, like Frank Crampton, who dropped in to call found the old man out of sorts. After some months he began to buy powder, fuse and dynamite caps.

One moonlight night the residents of Piute were shaken from their beds by an explosion over at Garlic Spring. Flames were rising high from the site. When they reached the scene of Old John's Castle, neither man nor house was there. Only the tracks of the buckboard and a burro heading north remained.

Months later two prospectors were crossing the floor of Death Valley just north of Furnace Creek when they came across the body of Old John Lamoigne. Apparently the old man, hating the new world he had built with his wealth, had headed back to his silver mine. Beside the buckboard lay the remains of his burro. The midsummer heat had killed them both. Even the most experienced men can be destroyed by the desert.

A rough-cut code of ethics existed among the desert miners. Claim-jumping was a cardinal crime. Following the tracks of another prospector unless he invited you was considered bad manners. Few grubstake agreements were put onto paper, yet prospectors who struck minerals rarely neglected to pay the grubstaker's third of their earnings.

When commercial mining started at a strike and miners worked for wages, some were not so careful about their honesty. A practice known as "high-grading" developed in the gold mines. As they shoveled ore into the carts, the miners came across small pieces of rock containing exceptionally high amounts of gold. These they slipped into their trouser cuffs or into concealed pockets beneath their shirts. After work they cashed in the ore to purchasers who specialized in this under-the-counter trade.

Some miners were making more money high-grading than in regular wages. When one company installed a changing room, where the miners had to change clothes under the eye of an inspector after leaving work, there was an uproar. "Unfair!" the miners complained. "We're being cheated!"

Soon "high-grading" became a slang word for stealing. Similarly the miner's phrase "deep enough," meaning that the hole had been drilled sufficiently, took on a slang meaning similar to "that's plenty." When a miner said dejectedly of his own affairs, "She's deep enough," he meant the same thing as a later generation which said, "I've had it."

Men and mines alike took on colorful names. Frequently the miner's nickname was based on his place of origin, like Nevada Bill or Montana Charley, or one of his personal characteristics. Cloudburst Pete acquired his moniker because of his misadventure with a flash flood. Cranky Casey was an unlucky prospector who grumbled that he "never found enough gold to fill a tooth."

Selection of names for mines and camps gave the miners an opportunity for fun. The gold boom town of Skidoo, born in 1905, took its name from the currently popular slang phrase, "Twenty-three—skidoo," a term of dismissal. The discovery, it seems, was made on the twenty-third of the month. The wealthy camp first known as Grandpa because its discoverers expected it to become "the grandpa of them all" later took on the more dignified name of Gold-field. Among the mines themselves were the Honeymoon, the Toughnut, the Elephant, the Lucky Cuss, the World Beater and the O. B. Joyful.

A desert man develops much skill in the art of survival. He comes to know the rock formations most likely to yield minerals, and sometimes more important, which are the possible sources of water holes. He learns which plants are edible, where he may safely take shortcuts and how to detect water undrinkable because of alkali. If he is in track-less desert without a compass, he knows a trick to help him find his directions. He uses his watch.

An oldtimer explained the trick this way, "Point the hour hand toward the sun. The point half-way between the hour hand and the twelve o'clock mark is due south. If it's cloudy, wet your thumbnail and stand a pencil on it. You're bound to get a shadow, and this will show you where the sun is."

As much a part of American desert lore as the rich strikes just mentioned are the "lost" mines. These are finds that have been made by prospectors, only to be lost from human grasp again by some unfortunate set of circum-stances before their wealth could be taken from the ground.

Some of these lost mines never existed except in men's imagination. As the years pass and the stories are repeated the wealth of these imaginary holes grows greater. For decades prospectors and city tenderfeet on vacations have been hunting the Lost Gunsight, Lost Pegleg, Lost Breyfogle and other fabled caches of riches, but without success.

Of all these missing desert mines, probably the most famous is the Lost Dutchman in the Superstition Mountains of southern Arizona. Unlike many, this one has a basis of fact and, indeed, a bloody history.

Back in the early 1870's two Germans named Jacob Walz and Jacob Wiser were prospecting together in Needle Canyon in the Superstitions. Surprising two men at work in a pit the Germans ruthlessly shot the miners in the back and seized samples of the ore. Back at their own campfire, they examined the rock specimens and were sure they contained high grade gold.

An idea came to the cold-blooded Walz. Why share these riches with anyone? When his partner turned his back momentarily, Walz shot him, too. These were the lawless days in Arizona territory when a man could disappear without raising much question. He could easily say his partner had been killed by Apache Indians.

Word that Walz had struck riches in the Superstitions spread through the Arizona settlements. Whenever he started back toward the mine, he was followed by goldhungry pursuers who wanted to break his secret. But he was a clever desert man, as well as a heartless killer, and

109

he always succeeded in evading them. For years Walz outsmarted them all, selling his sacks of ore in Phoenix or Tuscon for thousands of dollars.

Early in 1891, when the old Dutchman was nearly seventy, a sudden flood rolled down the Salt River at Phoenix, and the house of Jacob Walz was one of those swept away. Rescuers found him near death, but before he died he told his secret to two close friends, Julia Thomas and Reinhart Petrasch. He insisted that millions of dollars still remained in the mine.

Extremely excited, Julia Thomas and Petrasch set out for the Superstitions to find the fortune. They found nothing. For three months they searched without uncovering a trace. In fact they could not even locate most of the landmarks Walz had described. A few years earlier the area had been shaken by a heavy earthquake and there had been several cloudburst floods down the canyon. Perhaps these had changed the landmarks. Or perhaps the old man's memory had grown hazy.

Whatever the reason, the Lost Dutchman mine remains a mystery. For years fortune hunters by the hundreds have searched the Superstition Mountains. Dude ranches now make a game of it, taking their guests on a well-regulated search that turns into a western picnic with a chuck wagon and all the trimmings. But the mine must still be there somewhere. How else can those sacks of ore brought in by Jacob Walz be explained?

Putting aside the fascinating but elusive lost mines, the desert still hides millions of dollars in gold waiting to be mined. Partially worked mines hold ore that could be converted into thousands of dollars, and many other likely-looking claims have been staked but never developed.

If all this wealth is lying in the desert, why are so few people doing anything about it? Because most miners today cannot afford to dig gold.

The easy wealth near the surface has been seized by previous generations. What remains is mostly far underground. Expensive machinery is needed to reach and remove the gold, and the mining companies find their operating costs going higher and higher. In most cases they actually lose money by mining the precious metal.

In some streams men using placer pans just like the Forty-Niners still find "color." A few prospectors haul in valuable ore from their remote private diggings. An occasional commercial mine is working. But no longer is gold the magic wand that conjures up fabulous wealth.

The desert conceals the remains of her gold and silver treasure beneath sands and rocks, and few men today care enough to seek it. They are thinking instead about new kinds of desert mineral wealth.

8 The Desert's Magic Mineral

A test missile hurtles through space at more than 2,000 miles an hour. A shield of metallic material a quarter inch thick in the Atomic Energy Commission's plant at Oak Ridge, Tennessee, protects the workers from neutrons as effectively as a concrete wall of twenty-six inches. A substance hard enough to cut diamonds is subjected to heat so intense that the diamonds melt while the new material remains intact. A handful of fertilizer placed in the soil halts the cracking of celery stems and the internal rotting of sugar beets.

At first glance these achievements of American industry,

112

while impressive, seem to have nothing in common. Actually they and many other industrial marvels share a basic secret. All are made possible by the magic mineral, borax, which comes from a mammoth hole in the Mojave desert.

From above, the immense pit resembles the coiled loops of a giant's rope as the shadows fall across its cut-back terraces. In the bottom of the pit, 200 feet below the parched, dusty desert floor, an electric shovel bites off several tons of a whitish mineral and spills it into a waiting truck. The truck rumbles up the terraces and dumps its load into a crushing machine.

That cargo of ore is borax, kicked aside as a nuisance by the pioneers and now cherished by industry. The heat-drenched and trackless wastes over which the Death Valley survivors stumbled are yielding a versatile servant that aids men in a hundred ways. With it they make eyewash and soap powder, weed killers and fertilizers, glass and porcelain enamels. They put it into the gasoline of their automobiles for additional power.

Most spectacular of all, the basic element in borax, which chemists call boron, is being used to give jet fighters and missiles a valuable extra punch. The once-ignored mineral has become a national defense commodity of immense potential value.

All but a fraction of the free world's borax is being dug from the corner of the Mojave desert near Edwards Air Force Base in eastern California across which the pioneers plodded and suffered. The same dry lake beds whose shimmering mirages yielded no water for the thirsty emigrants, or at best a brackish alkaline fluid impossible to drink, today are producing huge quantities of borax.

The story goes back to a stone hut at a desert water hole some miles east of Death Valley, called Ash Meadows. The year was 1881. Aaron Winters and his Mexican-Indian wife, Rosie, grubbed out a hot, barren existence in their dirt-floored shack, and whenever a prospector happened along they extended their hospitality to him gladly. They were friendly folk and the desert was a lonely place.

A wandering prospector and his burro shambled up to their hut one night, seeking shelter. As they sat and talked, the visitor told Aaron and Rosie that he was not hunting gold or silver, but something white and crumbly called borax. Back east some factories and metal workers were asking for borax to use in their manufacturing.

"How can you tell when you find it?" Aaron asked.

The stranger explained that the samples should be mixed with certain chemicals and a match touched to them. If the sample burned green, it was borax. Apparently he left his host some of the alcohol and sulphuric acid needed for the test. The next morning he went on his way, a stray messenger of fate who changed the lives of Aaron and Rosie and many others.

Hardly believing what the prospector had told them about the worth of borax, Mr. and Mrs. Winters talked about the places around the desert where the mineral might be found. They loaded their burro and headed through a

gap in the mountains and down onto the torrid floor of Death Valley, camping at Furnace Creek, where the Forty-Niner emigrants had paused thirty years earlier. Rosie scooped up handfuls of the loose white substance that looked like balls of cotton while Aaron prepared for the test.

He dipped the cotton balls into the chemicals. Rosie and Aaron bent their heads close together over the material hopefully as he struck a match to it. Then joyful smiles spread across their dusty, sun-darkened faces.

Aaron let out a whoop that bounced all the way off the Funeral Mountains. "She burns green, Rosie!" he shouted. "We're rich!"

The valley floor around them as far as they could see was covered with the whitish substance. Suddenly it had turned into something desirable. Hundreds of miles away, in the cities, men wanted this borax. But without roads, how could Aaron and Rosie get the material out of Death

115

Valley? They couldn't load much on their old burro.

Aaron wrestled with the problem. For days the samples of borax waited in the cabin. Aaron learned that a rich man in San Francisco named W. T. Coleman was interested in the material. He sent some specimens to him.

Soon a representative of Coleman arrived at Death Valley and Aaron led him to the borax deposits.

"Will you sell your claim for $20,000?" the expert asked.

That was more money than Aaron and Rosie had earned in their entire lives. They readily accepted.

For the first time in history, the desolate floor of Death Valley was ready to yield something men desired. A borax company was organized and built the Harmony Borax Works near Furnace Creek.

But the puzzle that stumped Aaron Winters now faced the mining company. Gold and silver could be reduced to small bars of pure metal and carried in express boxes to the cities. But borax was a bulky commodity and must be supplied in large quantities to commercial users. The nearest railroad lay 165 miles to the west. Between stood mountains and arid basins without a drop of water except what could be coaxed from a handful of water holes, some of them more than fifty miles apart. In all this immensity of sand and rock there was not a house or structure of any sort, not even a dirt track good enough for a heavily loaded wagon to use. How could the borax be shipped across the dreary, treacherous space to the railroad?

The company called in an experienced freighter, J.W.S.

Perry, and asked him what he could do about it. "There isn't a road, so we'll build one. There aren't any wagons big enough to haul loads of borax, so let's make some—wagons so big that it will take twenty mules to pull a pair of them," he concluded.

Thus was born the twenty-mule-team borax route, one of the most rugged and adventurous chapters in the story of desert transportation. There were the 165 bone-dry miles to be covered, from Death Valley across the Panamints to the town of Mojave, with only three water holes on the entire route. In summer the temperatures along the wagon path hit 130 degrees. Sandstorms swept the desert, cutting the faces and hands of the drivers.

Most of the way, making a road consisted merely of driving a wagon over the route once and telling the other drivers, "Just follow the tracks." Here and there a few creosote bushes were cut out of the path. In the mountains, however, extensive grading was required before the borax wagons could maneuver up and down the slopes. Only one of the three water holes yielded moisture the year around. In the driest time of year, the drivers sometimes covered more than a hundred miles without finding a drop of water in the ground.

The wooden wagons Perry built to travel this route were marvels of durability. They had to be. Each was sixteen feet long, four feet wide and had sides six feet high. The back wheels were seven feet high, and each was protected by an iron tire eight inches wide and an inch thick. There was no cushion in them to ease the jostling.

117

The wagons were driven in pairs, one hooked behind the other. In the rear, like the caboose of a freight train, they dragged a twelve-hundred-gallon water tank on wheels. The total weight of this rig when loaded with borax was thirty-six tons, an enormous and unwieldy burden to be hauled along an unsurfaced, poorly graded trail.

Most remarkable of all were the mule teams which pulled these wagons. The twenty mules in each team were lined up in ten pairs. Only the two nearest the wagons, known as "wheelers," had a wagon tongue between them as a guide. The lead pair more than a hundred feet ahead were the only mules wearing bridles. The other sixteen mules were free except for a draw chain running the length of the procession, to which they were tied. Sometimes horses were used as wheelers instead of mules.

Each outfit was run by two men, a driver and his assistant, known as a "swamper." When the men climbed up on the wagons at Mojave and headed east for Death Valley, they faced at least twenty lonely days of bouncing across the desert at two miles an hour. Two or three times each way they passed other wagons, and there were men to talk with at the Harmony works in the valley. Otherwise they had only themselves and the mules for company.

Sitting on his high bench, the driver saw his team of twenty mules stretching out 120 feet ahead of him. He had no reins to guide them, only a huge whip with a twenty-two foot lash which he wielded with both hands. On the seat beside him was a box of small stones. These he hurled with the accuracy of a baseball pitcher at unruly mules beyond the reach of his whip.

The driver had two ways of passing his orders to the procession of mules. One was a picturesque flow of language which the intelligent animals seemed to understand. The other was a jerk line, a half-inch rope running forward through rings on the mules' collars to the bridles of the lead pair.

The company built station huts along the way, at the water holes and at dry camps between. Wagons headed east toward Death Valley carried loads of hay and grain for the animals and food supplies for the men. At each hut some supplies were dropped off for use by the westbound wagons.

The driver and his swamper carried extra food in case they had to camp on the open desert away from the established stations. They tried to time their journey so as to arrive at nightfall at one of the cabins, where they could roll into bunks for a good night's sleep. Breakdowns and delays frequently made this impossible. Eastbound the outfit could make twenty miles a day, but when headed out of Death Valley with a load of borax, sixteen miles was the usual pace. Much of the time the men were smothered in dust kicked up by the mules.

When mules and men were in tune, things usually went well enough. But if they got at cross purposes the result was chaos. So long and unwieldy were the twenty-mule teams that getting them and the wagons around sharp bends in the mountain canyons required feats of skill and colorful persuasion by the drivers.

119

"Going down grade with a full load was the worst," one old-time driver said. "Because of the way the wagons were hitched up, the mules couldn't hold the load back, like a single team could do on ordinary wagons, so we had to depend entirely on the brake levers.

"Everything was all right if the brakes held. But once in awhile a brake block would give way or a rod pull out and then there was trouble. The only thing to do then was to get the mules going on a trot or a gallop if the wagons got rollin' too fast, and try to keep the mules from gettin' run down by the wagons until you got to a place where you you could swing 'em off the road and up the side of a hill or into a sandy place where you could get the wagons stopped."

Sometimes a wheel would strike a rock as the mules galloped to escape from being run down and crushed by the thirty-six tons of wood and borax. The wagons would tip over on the desert with a splintering crunch. Borax spilled in profusion on the ground.

Frequently the driver and his swamper on the mules were injured. There was no help to be summoned. If the two men could not get the wagons upright again, there was nothing for them to do but camp beside the wreckage and wait, perhaps two days or more, before another wagon came along.

Living and working so intimately, week after week, the driver and his swamper often fell into bitter arguments. They quickly ran out of things to talk about. Petty annoyances grew into subjects for angry quarreling. One crew arrived in Mojave after three weeks on the desert barely speaking to each other because of an argument over the way the swamper wore his hat.

The task of gathering the cotton ball mineral was done by Chinese laborers. Pushing two-wheeled carts across the jagged crust of the borax beds, they were protected only a little from the murderous heat by their broad coolie hats. The pure borax was crystallized into chunks for loading in the twenty-mule-team wagons. As the feverishly hot days of midsummer approached, and the temperature stayed steadily above 120 degrees, the chemical process of crystallization would not work. No borax could be produced. The entire operation had to be shut down each summer.

Discoveries of borax deposits were made outside Death Valley, where the heat was less and transportation easier. For many years borax was shipped by a narrow gauge railroad to a connecting rail point known as Death Valley Junction. Time and deterioration of the mines ended the life of both railroads, and many a campfire has been built from their ties. Death Valley Junction today is a sleepy settlement far out in the desert without a railroad track of any kind to justify its name.

At one point before any borax railroad was built, the mining company tried using a steam tractor to do the job of the twenty-mule teams. "Old Dinah" was faster than the mules on level ground, but on the hills she was all but useless. More than once the coal-gobbling steam engine had to be pulled from the sand by the mules she was supposed to replace. In disgust she was sold to a gold min-

121

ing company. Today "Old Dinah" stands in all her rusty glory at the entrance to Furnace Creek Ranch.

Borax has a history going back 4,000 years, and was one of the strange substances brought back to Europe from Asia by Marco Polo in the thirteenth century. But its uses were still limited at the time of the discoveries in the American desert. Borax was used to improve the glaze of pottery, for cleansing purposes, softening water and processing fine metals. Boric acid served as an eyewash. Recently researchers have found immense new possibilities.

Boron, the basic element found in borax, does not appear as a free element in nature, but always in combination with other materials from which it must be separated. But borax, first experimented with in combination with oxygen and more recently with hydrogen, nitrogen, phosphorus and arsenic, has produced amazing results.

Work on boron fuel for jet airplanes and missiles has been covered with secrecy for security reasons. However, it is known that such fuel may extend the range of supersonic aircraft and missiles by forty per cent beyond that provided by the older type fuels made from petroleum. Already a test missile burning a boron compound fuel has traveled more than three times the speed of sound, or faster than 2,000 miles an hour. A round-the-world flight nonstop without refueling by a U.S. Air Force bomber using boron became a possibility.

The heavier the load of fuel a jet plane or missile must carry, the more limited its range. Hydrogen is considered the perfect fuel, but its extremely high combustion rate creates an explosion hazard. Boron may be the answer. Extremely light and itself producing heat, it combines with hydrogen into a liquid or solid form that can be transported safely.

Boron is being examined for use in plastics for aircraft. Extreme speed and high altitudes demand materials with flexibility over a range of temperatures from below zero to a thousand degrees above zero. Combined with phosphorus and with arsenic, boron has given encouraging results.

When made into boron nitride, the versatile desert mineral forms borazon, a substance hard enough to scratch a diamond—a significant discovery for manufacturers of industrial tools.

Dozens of other uses for the borax family are in operation or under development. A borate powder mixed with water is dropped from airplanes to check forest fires. Borax is used in fibre glass, which is spun into threads and woven into cloth. The widespread use of procelain enamel in kitchens and bathrooms is possible because borax prevents excessive warping of the enamelware. A substance called boral, made of aluminum and boron carbide, is being used as a shield against neutrons in atomic energy operations.

"Is there enough borax to do all these jobs?" is a natural question. The answer, happily, is yes. Almost unlimited supplies lie in the Mojave desert waiting to be mined.

The huge open pit mine of the United States Borax and Chemical Company at Boron, California, taps a mass of borax two miles long, a half mile wide and more than 200 feet deep. Sixty miles to the northeast, another wealth of borax is being pumped from beneath the muddy ooze of Searles Lake by two other companies.

The riches of the American desert have had a heavy influence in the world for more than a century. Its gold and silver have created objects of beauty, been minted into coins and swayed the country's economy and politics. Now the magic mineral, borax, is opening vistas of new products and supersonic travel as enthralling as the desert horizon itself—almost unlimited, exciting in its vastness and tinged with the mystery of what lies beyond.

9 Stagecoaches Rolling!

The chance presence of springs saves Vallecito, lying on the western edge of the sun-drenched Colorado desert a few miles north of the Mexican border, from being as parched and dreary as the country around it.

A single low adobe building dozes in the midst of the snug green oasis reached by a sandy track which passes for a road. Nobody has lived there for a great many years. When the mercury hangs at 115 degrees, the thick clay walls provide a cool haven from the desert's torments. Once in a while an automobile bounces along the dirt road from the north and its curious occupant stops beneath the trees. But hardly ever in summer does a motorist risk the

125

sketchy trail across the desert from the south.

Vallecito is sleeping through the twentieth century. A hundred years ago things were different.

The men at Vallecito saw a small cloud of dust moving across the desert toward them from the south. Gradually it grew, and from it emerged the outline of four horses running at the front of a stagecoach.

Careening to a halt outside the adobe station, the driver jumped from his seat. Through the heavy layer of dust on the coach door the words "Overland Mail Company" were barely visible.

"Hurry up and change those horses," the driver urged. "We're running behind schedule. We've hauled this mail all the way from St. Louis and we don't want to be late getting it to San Francisco. Not on the very first trip across the desert by the Butterfield Overland Mail!"

The Butterfield coach which paused at Vallecito that early October day in 1858 rolled swiftly northwestward to San Francisco. Early on Sunday morning, October 10, it raced over cobblestone streets to the post office in that gold-crazy boom town, coach horn blowing wildly, and unloaded its precious cargo of mail. Just half an hour less than twenty-four days had elapsed since those pouches left St. Louis!

At last the west coast was linked to the rest of the United States by a regularly scheduled mail and passenger route. Mail service had penetrated the desert barrier.

From the day the first men had come to the dry lands several thousand years ago, travel has been among the most challenging problems of American desert existence.

At first men moved around very little. The early Indians found a patch of ground where they could scratch out a living, and seldom traveled more than a few miles away. They had no horses or beasts of burden. When they went anywhere across the hot, dry lands they walked.

White men are a roving lot, however. Even on the desert they wanted to see what lay beyond the next hill. Slowly they developed a few basic trails across the empty spaces, following river valleys where possible and setting their course with an eye to the water holes. But there were some stretches to be crossed where there was no water—as much as a hundred miles, perhaps, without a drop of moisture. Such was their determination and their desire to go places that they plunged ahead, anyway. They gambled their lives that they could reach the next known water hole—frequently a stagnant pool almost hidden beneath the sand—before their endurance failed and their canteens ran dry.

The southern trail across New Mexico, Arizona and the Colorado desert of Southern California was the driest and hottest of all. It was not a road, as the people of today know roads, but a set of footprints, hoof marks and wagon wheel tracks pounded into a path. Mile after mile it stretched across the wastelands, sometimes for long distances without a curve, other places twisting and turning to avoid quicksands, mountains, sand dunes and other natural barriers. Modern roadmakers blast obstacles out of their way; the early desert trailmakers tried to go around as many as possible.

In its swift desert crossing the Butterfield stage had followed this historic southern route—a path traveled by Spanish priests afoot, conquistadors on horses, trappers on mules, invading American soldiers, emigrant wagon trains, Apache Indian raiders and huge cattle droves. Pioneer motorists crossed it later on a sand-swept road of wooden planks. Today a stream of sleek, chromium-trimmed automobiles race seventy miles an hour along a broad paved highway.

The desert is the same as always, but American mechanical skill at building roads and vehicles has tamed it.

In the 1850's the bustling new state of California was demanding that the federal government do something about giving it some proper mail service.

"We're part of the Union now," the Californians argued. "We don't want to wait six weeks for letters and news from New York to come by ship, all the way around by Panama. Give us a stagecoach route!"

Finally the government heeded this plea. It gave John Butterfield, an old-time freighter experienced in desert travel, a contract to run a stagecoach line from St. Louis to San Francisco, more than 2,700 miles. The mail was to go through twice a week in each direction, and every trip was to be made in twenty-five days or less.

That made speed essential. Every twenty miles in green areas, and wherever possible in the desert, station huts were built where fresh horses could be hitched to the stagecoach. Some of these lonely stations in mid-desert were hundreds of miles from a town and had only the water that could be hauled from the nearest wells.

A solitary passenger made the first westward trip on the Butterfield stage. Waterman L. Ormsby, a correspondent for the New York *Herald,* rode the entire distance from St. Louis to San Francisco and endured enough jolting and bouncing to last him a lifetime. His dispatches to his newspaper provide lively glimpses of pioneer desert travel.

"We finally got under way again and pursued our weary course along the edge of a plain, thumping and bumping at a rate which threatened not to leave a whole bone in my body. What with the dust and the sun pouring directly on our heads . . . I found the day's ride most unpleasant, and at several of our camps readily availed myself of the opportunity to plunge into the Pecos, muddy as it was."

He describes seeing the bones of animals and men strewn across the dreary Staked Plains, "their grim skeletons warning the traveler of the dreadful dangers of the desert."

Twelve years before the first Butterfield stagecoach rumbled across the southern desert trail, General Stephen W. Kearny had led the U.S. Army of the West along this same desolate route. The year was 1846, and the war between the United States and Mexico had begun. The general's orders were to march his small force of 120 men across the desert to California and conquer that region from the Mexicans.

As the Spaniards had learned three centuries earlier, an

129

army on the march across the desert faces extreme hardships. Kearny's men suffered severely. Their wagons had to be abandoned because they moved so slowly through the heavy sand, and the blue-clad soldiers pressed ahead on horses and mules. The artillery pieces the animals were pulling frequently bogged down in the soft ground. Soon thirst, hunger and the heavy burdens crippled the animals. Most of the soldiers were forced to dismount and walk in straggling disorder. Travel on the desert was not easy.

It was an exhausted force that slowly dragged itself along, knowing that after crossing the desert it must march straight into battle. With eyes sore with dust that had hung like a cloud all day over their procession, the soldiers camped along the Gila River in Arizona. Here they encountered that desert phenomenon where the ground seemed to be covered with frost on a day when the temperature was in the nineties. Wherever a man or animal stepped the barren soil became moist, as the salts of the earth rose to the surface.

At last the struggling army reached the Colorado River, fording it at Yuma crossing, one of the crucial places on the southern desert trail. Plunging into the dreaded Colorado desert, their proud uniforms ragged and torn, the men scrambled with great difficulty through the huge sand dunes only to come out onto a treeless expanse of hard-packed clay on which the heat waves shimmered. Men and animals alike were growing desperate for water.

But General Kearny was determined, and his small company of fighters finally passed Vallecito and reached the broad green valley of Warner's ranch, owned by an American settler in the coastal mountains. Here food and water were plentiful. After a brief rest the American forces pushed forward and met the Californians in sharp battle. The tattered, ill-fed desert marchers were in no condition to fight. But they had their orders: Conquer California! Eighteen men of the small force were killed, and it looked for a time as though the long, miserable desert crossing had been made only to encounter disaster.

Under cover of darkness three men set forth to walk through the enemy lines and summon help from the U.S. Navy in San Diego, thirty miles away. Kit Carson, the famous scout; Lieutenant Beale, who later led the U.S. Camel Corps, and his Indian servant crept barefoot through the cactus, thorns and rocks and delivered their message. Reinforcements came from the warships in San Diego, the Californians were defeated and California fell into American hands. The hazardous trek over the barely discernible desert trail had not been in vain.

Throughout the last half of the nineteenth century still another peril lurked along the southern desert trail: Apache Indian raiders.

The Apaches were ruthless fighters who killed without mercy. They had been deceived and betrayed by white men, and under such skillful leaders as Mangus Colorado (Red Sleeves), Cochise and Geronimo they terrorized the southern desert and mountains for several decades.

Among the most vicious of the Apache raids was the

131

massacre of the Oatman family in 1851. This family had foolishly pushed on ahead of its emigrant wagon train west of Tucson. Their food had run low and they were anxious to reach Yuma crossing. The red men approached, apparently peacefully. Then, without warning, they fell upon the lone party, killing six of the family of nine.

The Indians plundered the wagons, seized the oxen and rode off to their desert hiding place. With them they took the two Oatman daughters, teen-age Olive and her younger sister, Mary Ann. Lorenzo, a boy of fifteen, was rolled over a cliff and left for dead. Later, miraculously recovering his strength, he managed to reach a friendly Pima Indian village.

For several years, Lorenzo's mission in life was to rescue his sisters, and eventually his perseverance was rewarded. Although Mary Ann had died in captivity, Olive and her brother were reunited and returned to the North, leaving the desert and its horrible experiences behind them forever.

As long as the southern desert trail has existed, the Yuma crossing of the Colorado where the Oatmans met such tragic disaster has been a dominant place. Its history is rich in blood-tingling episodes. Competition for the ferry service was keen, and many are the stories of revengeful murder as both white man and Indian fought for control.

The U.S. Army built Fort Yuma on the hilltop overlooking the river where once a Spanish mission had stood.

Paddlewheel steamboats brought supplies from the Gulf of California, a hundred miles below.

The town of Yuma, on the Arizona side of the river, had a strange beginning. The men who ran the Yuma ferry charged very high prices; travelers either had to pay or swim, and swimming was difficult and dangerous.

Two American civil engineers arrived at the east bank of the river one day, but did not have the twenty-five-dollar fee the ferry operator demanded. Unpacking their surveying instruments, they went to work laying out a town site on the banks of the river. They marked streets and squares, put up location flags to indicate choice waterfront lots and drew an elaborate map of their new town.

All this activity made the ferry proprietor curious. Excited by the chance to get a real estate bargain, and worried about competition for his ferry, the boatman examined the map and chose what looked to him like the finest lot.

When informed that the cost would be twenty-five dollars, the boatman thought a moment. "Tell you what I'll do," he said. "I'll ferry you and all your equipment across the river in exchange for that lot."

The shrewd travelers quickly accepted, were ferried over the river without spending a penny and headed across the desert toward the Pacific. They had sold the gullible ferry operator a piece of sandy soil they did not own. Years passed before a town developed on the site they had surveyed.

When automobiles became popular in the years before

134

the first World War, a new phase developed in the life of the southern desert trail.

Some of the worst perils had been conquered. The Apaches had been rounded up and put on a reservation. Settlements had been established and deep wells dug, so that water was no longer a critical problem for those travelers who had the wisdom to stay on the main road and carry a reserve supply. But the desert surface was too soft to support the small hard tires of the early automobiles. Horses, mules, stagecoaches, ox-drawn wagons, yes; but not the spinning wheels of a four-cylinder car. Especially in the massive sand dunes west of Yuma—dunes which have since been the setting for many Hollywood films about the Foreign Legion and other stories supposedly located on the Sahara desert—motoring was impossible.

Once again ingenious men found an answer. Lumber was cut in the coastal mountains of California, hauled to the desert and hammered into parallel tracks two feet wide, set at the width of automobile wheels. Bundled in long linen dusters, caps and goggles, the adventurous drivers steered their high-wheeled open cars cautiously along the plank paths toward Yuma. Turnouts were built at intervals, in case an oncoming car was encountered. There was so little traffic that this seldom happened.

Later a roadway of solid planking, cross-ties bound together with iron bands, replaced the tracks. The planking was assembled in thirty-foot sections and hauled into place by teams of horses. When a heavy windstorm shifted the sand dunes, road workers simply dragged the plank sections into new positions to take advantage of the altered terrain. Not until 1924 did an oiled road replace the old plank highway.

Usually the cars traveled in groups, so the drivers could help each other in case of a breakdown. In the back of his car each motorist carried extra cans of gasoline and water, firearms and shovels to dig the car out of the sand if it slipped off the road.

Today motorists racing along the gently graded pavement of U.S. Highway 80, from San Diego on the Pacific coast eastward through Arizona and New Mexico, follow closely along the historic southern desert trail. Off to the side of the highway, half buried in the sand dunes, they can see sections of the old plank road slowly decaying in the heat.

At Yuma they cross the Colorado on a long bridge. And on the hill above, where the Spanish mission and later Fort Yuma stood, they see a different kind of structure—an Indian school. Here the federal government teaches the Indians the white man's culture and how to live in the modern civilization that has swept across their desert lands along this ancient, tortured route.

10 Death Valley Scotty's Castle

The sound of chimes rings on the desert. Fifty miles from the nearest town, with nothing in sight but dreary, gravel-strewn ground and rocky hills, the music of a carillon like that in some great cathedral fills the dry air. What kind of a phenomenon is this?

The traveler swings his car atop the crest of a hill at the northern end of Death Valley and sees a concrete bell tower pointing into the sky. A few yards further and the entire picture is revealed: a palatial Spanish castle worth millions of dollars rises majestically in the middle of the thirsty wastelands.

This is Death Valley Scotty's castle. In many respects it is the most fantastic, illogical and baffling building in the United States.

Why should anybody spend millions to build a spectacular castle in such a remote and barren corner of the desert? Everyone who comes to see the structure asks this question. Nobody has the full answer, and nobody ever will. The fabulous old man who could have told, but wouldn't, is buried on a knoll overlooking the castle and the sweep of desert beyond. Death Valley Scotty spun thousands of tales in his eighty-one years, many of them whoppers, but he never revealed the complete story of his castle.

For half a century Scotty was the best known man on the American desert. People of the faraway eastern cities read in their Sunday papers about his escapades and his castle in remote Death Valley. His name was a household word from coast to coast. When he came to the city and scattered hundred-dollar bills around the hotels and streets like scraps of wastepaper, he was followed by curious, greedy crowds. In his ten-gallon cowboy hat, blue flannel shirt and flaming red necktie he was a flamboyant figure who looked more at home in the wide desert spaces than on the city pavements.

"How did you get to be so rich?" the city people asked.

"Nothing to it. Found me a gold mine, that's all," Scotty drawled. Always people wanted to know where his mine was located. Scotty just grinned and shrugged them off.

Death Valley Scotty's first big publicity splash occurred

when he breezed into Los Angeles from his desert cabin and took suites in three different hotels. "Maybe a couple of them will be noisy. A fellow gets used to quiet out there on the desert," he explained in his booming voice.

He tipped hotel bellboys by handing them halves of fifty-dollar bills, then buying back the useless portions for twenty dollars. He lit cigars with five-dollar bills, threw money into the gutters for boys to scramble after and, to satisfy those who wondered about the source of his money, carried along a bag of gold nuggets.

By the time Scotty died at his castle in 1954, the truth had come out. Death Valley Scotty's mansion did not really belong to him, and never had. Scotty was just a yarn-spinning desert character with a wealthy benefactor who furnished most of the money for Scotty's stunts and his castle for the fun of it. The friend was Albert M. Johnson, a Chicago insurance executive, and probably the nearest thing to a walking gold mine that ever lived.

Fifty miles north of Furnace Creek Ranch, isolated at the upper end of Death Valley, Grapevine Canyon leads down from the mountains. The altitude is 2,000 feet, compared with the below-sea-level readings down in the heart of the valley, and the weather is correspondingly cooler. Only two things would normally attract men to this remote desert spot, the spacious view and the small stream trickling down the canyon.

A ramshackle cabin at the mouth of Grapevine Canyon was the only building for many miles around, fifty years ago. In it lived a slick-tongued prospector named Walter Scott, who had been hanging around the desert after a youthful career as a cowboy in Buffalo Bill's Wild West show back East.

Periodically Scott, whom the world came to know as Death Valley Scotty, emerged from his desert hideout. He tossed around money and big stories with abandon. Then he disappeared again up Grapevine Canyon.

What the world did not know was that part of the time there was another occupant of the cabin—Johnson. The wealthy Chicagoan with the odd sense of humor had been hurt in a railroad wreck and had come to the desert for his health. Scotty, who knew the ways of desert life, took Johnson under his wing. An unusual friendship grew up between the rich city man and the prospector who talked big.

One day a freight wagon rumbled down the dirt track of Grapevine Canyon from the old Tonopah and Tidewater desert railroad, twenty miles away, and dumped a load of lumber. Another came with sacks of cement.

Dozens of workmen and mountains of material arrived. Soon the noise of hammers and concrete mixers echoed in the canyon. A fabulous castle of turrets and patios, huge tiled rooms and intricate iron grillwork rose on the desert. So much building material was hauled down the deeply rutted dirt road that the hubs of the wagons scraped the ground.

Soon the desert grapevine was buzzing. Scotty ran an advertisement in a Nevada newspaper asking, "Will all my friends and enemies stay away from the shack until done?"

Furnishings and paintings were imported at great cost. A magnificent pipe organ was installed in the music room. The main reception room, almost big enough to house a basketball game, has rugs of deep pile brought from Spain, so valuable that visitors to the castle wear cloth shoe coverings to protect them. The gigantic dining room table of solid black walnut weighs 1,200 pounds. The fabulous "castle" was, and still is, an incongruous sight on the desert's face.

Just as fabulous were the stunts Scotty delighted in. One day he walked into the Santa Fe railroad office in Los Angeles and announced, "I want to hire a train to Chicago. Make it the fastest train you can put together, because I'm going to break the speed record from Los Angeles to Chicago." The Santa Fe was glad enough to have the publicity, especially since Scotty had showed that he could pay for the unheard-of stunt. They cleared the 2,200 miles of track to give the "Coyote Special" full speed ahead.

This was in 1905, when trains still were pulled by huge steam locomotives. Pouring out black smoke, the four-car "Special" roared out of the Los Angeles station, headed east as fast as its wheels would turn. Through the coastal mountains it climbed, then raced across the Mojave desert, climbed through the Raton Pass and across the prairies to Chicago.

Scotty and his small group of guests held a cross-country party in their private train. Part of the time the prospector sat up in the locomotive with the engineer. As the "Coyote Special" raced through the towns along the route, word of its progress was flashed around the country. Scotty had made sure the newspapers heard of his plans. Nineteen locomotives were used along the run in relays, the way horses had been changed on the old Butterfield stagecoach. At times the careening locomotive and its swaying cars reached a speed of 110 miles an hour.

Climbing down from the Pullman car in Chicago's Dearborn Street station, Scotty waved his cowboy hat at the crowd and shouted, "Whoopie doodle! We did it! Forty-four hours and fifty-four minutes. That's thirteen hours faster than anybody's ever come from Los Angeles before."

His train had set a record that lasted for nearly thirty years, but it had not cost him anything like the hundred thousand dollars that he claimed. A receipt from the Santa Fe shows that the train rental actually cost $5,500. Scotty rarely let the truth get in the way of a good story.

Scotty talked so big about his gold mine that several people tried to call his bluff. A New York banker who had given him a grubstake early in his career believed that he was entitled to part of the mine's profits—if there really was a mine.

He dispatched some mining engineers from the East and sent word to Scotty that he must show them the mine. The result was a weird chapter in desert history known as the Battle of Windy Gap.

The easterners got off the train at Barstow, 150 miles

outh of Death Valley. Scotty was there to meet them with
a string of burros and a supply wagon. The astonished
desert newcomers saw that the wagon had armor plate on
its sides and a stack of rifles. Guards carrying rifles and six-
shooters surrounded the wagon.

The visitors were alarmed. "Is the trip into the desert
that dangerous?" they asked.

Scotty shrugged nonchalantly. "Don't let it worry you.
Piutes on the warpath. Their chief, old Dripping Knife,
claims my gold belongs to them."

This was more than the easterners had bargained for.
But they climbed aboard the wagon and started north
across the desert toward Death Valley. At Wingate Pass,
through which the old twenty-mule teams used to emerge
from the valley, Scotty warned his guests that they were
in dangerous territory.

Suddenly the worried visitors heard war whoops. Out
from behind bushes, up from the gulches and down from
the hills came what looked to them like a swarm of red-
skins. The attackers galloped toward the wagon, yelling
and firing their guns. Scotty's guards fired back, just like
a western movie today. The eastern engineers jumped out
of the wagon, crawled on their stomachs to the nearest
gulch and hid until the shooting ended.

Scotty found them crouching there and proclaimed jovi-
ally, "We drove them off that time. You fellows ready to
go ahead?"

"Let's go back to Barstow," their leader said. "We'll
take your word about the mine." Not until several days

143

later did they discover that the fight was a fake, arranged by Scotty to discourage their investigation.

There is something about the desert that makes the tales grow tall. Perhaps when they sit around campfires and talk, men are trying to keep pace with the hugeness of their surroundings. Clear air and open spaces make the imagination soar. It becomes difficult to determine where the truth ends and yarn-spinning begins, especially when the storyteller was Scotty.

Bit by bit his relationship with Johnson became known, yet public knowledge of his friendship with the wealthy Chicagoan did not keep Scotty from bragging about his secret mine. Johnson had fun hanging around the fringe of Scotty's operations in disguise. He was present at the Battle of Windy Gap as a Doctor Jones.

A lawsuit failed to produce evidence that Scotty really had a mine, and Johnson testified, "Scotty hasn't got a dime. I've been paying his bills for years. He paid me back in laughs."

In his later years Scotty spent most of his time at the castle. Thousands of visitors every year made the long, lonesome drive from Tonopah or Furnace Creek to inspect the luxurious structure, to which they paid a dollar admission. The first question their friends asked when they returned home was, "Did you see Scotty?"

Some did, and thought themselves lucky. The old fellow didn't live in his castle—"too fancy for my tastes" —but had a small cabin nearby. Once or twice a day he

came to the castle, settled in his favorite chair and put himself on show for the tourists. Then the flow of stories began, and who could tell how much was the truth?

One night a starry-eyed city woman asked to hear about one of his adventures.

The old prospector looked at her seriously, then told about the time he was walking along a rocky desert ledge with his mule, hunting for gold. Scotty stopped to look around, and when he was ready to go again his mule could not move.

"No matter how hard I pushed, that critter just stood there. Beatin' him didn't work, either. I went around to his head, so's I could put a blindfold on him. When I stepped onto that ledge, I couldn't move either. My feet were clamped down tight."

The visitor asked in awe, "What was the trouble?"

"Lady, that rock was so full of minerals that it was magnetized. The magnetic pull was holding the mule's shoes and it had grabbed hold of the hobnails in my boots. Finally I wiggled out of my shoes and walked back to camp in my stockings." Scotty shook his head sorrowfully as he thought of that mule. "Poor critter," he said. "I couldn't do a thing for him. Just had to leave him in the desert. I guess he's still stuck out there on that ledge."

Although Scotty is gone, his spirit still hovers over Grapevine Canyon. Fifty thousand visitors drive to the castle every year and wonder at its magnificence. Looking down at them from the red tile roof is a metal weather-

146

ane depicting Scotty frying bacon over a desert campfire.

Before Johnson, the real owner, died he gave the castle o the Gospel Foundation of California. The dollars paid by tourists to visit this luxurious structure in the depth of he desert are used by the Foundation to pay for charitable work.

The desert is changing and adopting modern ways. No onger is it home for flamboyant tricksters like Death Valley Scotty, because they are too easily debunked. While he ived, however, Scotty was the symbol of adventurous, ree-handed life, known by reputation to millions all over he world. His peculiar castle is a lonely monument to older, wilder days on the American desert.

11 Conquering the Colorado

A geographer drawing a map of the American desert does not have to worry much about marking in the rivers, because there are so few of them. Although hundreds of stream beds and canyons crisscross this parched area of the United States, most of these hold water only a few weeks a year; some, only a few hours.

The Colorado River is by far the greatest of the desert rivers. Among the giant streams of the United States it is the most spectacular, the most perilous and the loneliest, a turbulent mass of water rolling in a deep channel through a thirsty land.

For centuries this torrent poured unchecked through

148

canyons and sand-swept plains, carrying its muddy waters from the Rocky Mountains to the Gulf of California. It contributed little to the desert, beyond watering a few fertile lowland stretches where Indian tribes could raise their crops. And it took little except silt from a land which has no water to spare. The river happened to be *in* the desert, because that area lay athwart its path to the sea. But it never was part of the desert, the way the rivers of more fertile regions are.

Then men with spectacular plans and engineers with modern tools met the challenge of this gigantic waste of the desert's most needed resource. They tamed the Colorado, until today the river is the servant of the land. Its waters are life-giving fluid for millions of Americans who reside on and near the southwestern desert. The conquest of the Colorado is an exciting chapter in the story of America's arid regions—an epic of ingenuity, vision, extreme danger and a half century of hard work.

The Spanish explorers called the river "Colorado," their word for red. Its waters ran reddish-brown with the sands of the desert. Along its treacherous 1,500-mile course southwestward from the high Rockies, through the Grand Canyon and then south to the Gulf through the heat-drenched core of the desert, it accumulates the drainage of seven states. Few people live along the river's banks even today; many portions of its shore have been scantily explored.

The king of the desert rivers was largely a mystery, except in its lower reaches, when Lieutenant Joseph C. Ives piloted his small stern wheel steamer, *Explorer,* upstream a hundred years ago.

The Lieutenant's orders from the War Department were simple: to see how far up the river he could navigate, and to gather information for the growing number of westward-bound emigrants. Could the Colorado be used as a desert waterway for hauling supplies?

After much difficulty, Ives and his crew assembled the *Explorer* on the sand flats at the Colorado's mouth, from parts which had been shipped from Philadelphia around by Panama. They steamed north to Fort Yuma, causing much excitement in that lonely outpost, and ultimately inched their way 400 miles upstream.

But the voyage of the *Explorer* was a torment of grounding on sandbars and fighting through rapids and sandstorms. Nothing went right. The Indians who lived along the lower river valley enjoyed seeing the fire-spitting monster in trouble and knew exactly where to gather for the fun. The sight of assembled Indians caused moans from the crew, because they knew it was a sure sign of a dangerous sandbar ahead.

Disaster ended the expedition when the *Explorer* crashed at full speed into a submerged rock, just as it neared Black Canyon. Anxious to see just a little more, Lieutenant Ives took the ship's rowboat on upstream through the narrow gap between the walls of the canyon. Fifty feet above the river he saw driftwood caught in the reddish-black volcanic rocks, indicating the height to which the Colorado's torrents rose during the spring floods.

Something far loftier was destined to rise on those canyon walls than the driftwood hanging above the explorer's head. Lieutenant Ives was at the exact place where seventy-five years later the highest dam in the world was to be built. It is the site of Hoover Dam, whose construction made the conquest of the Colorado River a reality and helped bend the desert to man's will.

At the opening of the twentieth century this vast resource still had not been harnessed or made useful to man. Potentially the sandy wastes of California's southernmost portion, covered with tons of silt deposit, were some of the richest farming land in the United States. All that was needed to make the desert bloom was water. And there was the broad Colorado River flowing across the desert, its waters going to waste in the Gulf of California a few miles to the south.

Men of imagination asked, "Why not cut an irrigation ditch from the river and drain off part of its flow onto the fertile desert?" Since the river was higher than the desert's center, known as the Salton sink, the water would flow out by gravity once a channel was cut. A simple idea, but an extremely dangerous one, as the dreamers were to find out to their immense cost and sorrow.

Dr. Oliver Wozencraft, one of the Forty-Niners, was the first man to propose irrigating the Colorado desert. He did not live to see his plan realized, but at the turn of the century a newer generation took up his idea. A diversion canal was cut through the Colorado's banks on the west side of the river near Yuma. The first drops of water flowed onto the parched lands in May, 1901, and within a few months crops were gathered. The Imperial Valley was born.

Settlers flocked in by every train, a land boom flourished and the rich desert soil which had never felt a plow was yielding several crops a year. Cotton, alfalfa, vegetables and melons in profusion were being shipped from the valley. The dream had come true, or so it seemed.

But the engineers and the farmers had not reckoned sufficiently with the Colorado's bag of tricks. They were trying to make the untamed and temperamental creature work for them without first putting a harness on it.

The heading structure at the diversion canal outlet offered an attractive target for the silt accumulated over more than a thousand miles above the Valley. Soon it was clogged, and the irrigation company did a dangerous thing. They made an open cut in the river bank to bypass the clogged heading structure until the sandy plug could be removed from it. The farmers got their water that winter of 1904 all right, but the river had its revenge.

Early in 1905 the mountain snows far upstream in the Rockies flooded the river and engulfed farms which had been reclaimed from the desert. Uncontrolled currents swept into the saucer-shaped area, and a lake was formed, known as the Salton Sea.

By spring of the next year, the situation had become extremely serious. Part of Mexicali, the town on the southern side of the U. S.-Mexico border, was undermined and swept away. Calexico, on the American side, was under heavy threat. Water lapped at the tracks of the Southern Pacific Railroad's main east-west line which crossed the Imperial Valley. The ultimate peril was that the entire Valley would disappear under 300 feet of ocean water as the Gulf of California surged back onto the desert, just as in ancient times.

The most skillful engineering and construction men available were ordered to use every possible resource to get the runaway river under control. The Southern Pacific was willing to foot the bill. All through the summer of 1906 the men struggled vainly to build a dam of brush and rock across the river.

E. H. Harriman, president of the railroad, appealed to President Theodore Roosevelt for help. The reply was to save the Imperial Valley; the government would help pay the cost.

What followed was a supreme effort born of desperation. In fifteen days, 80,000 cubic yards of rock and gravel cascaded into the gap. In February, 1907, the engineers announced, "We've done it!" The breach was closed and the valley saved after a fight of two years.

The Colorado was controlled but it was not yet conquered. The agricultural wealth of the desert could never be called safe until a large dam was built far upstream to control the river's flow and prevent floods from developing. To be financially possible, the dam also must be a source of electric power which could be generated from the river's waters and sold to customers.

There are not many customers for electricity in an empty desert, so for two decades the situation remained unchanged. The people of the Imperial Valley kept a worried eye on the levees during the high waters each year.

The solution finally was found not on the desert itself, but 250 miles away in Southern California. The growing population of Los Angeles and the surrounding towns needed more electricity than could easily be produced nearby. Far-seeing men agreed to purchase a large portion of the electricity if the federal government built a dam.

With this assurance plus an agreement among the seven

states of the river's basin concerning proportionate rights to its waters, action finally came. In 1928 the Boulder Dam Project bill was written into law. The American people were setting out to conquer the desert's greatest river at last.

The site chosen for the dam was Black Canyon, where Lieutenant Ives' expedition met with disaster. This was to be no mere barrier of concrete across a canyon, but an immensely complex structure with four major purposes —water storage, flood control, silt control and generation of electric energy.

The designs that came off the drawing boards are an engineering marvel. This is the highest dam in the world, rising 726 feet above bedrock, as high as a sixty-story skyscraper. At its base the barrier is 660 feet thick, more than the length of two normal city blocks. As the dam rises it becomes thinner, until at the two-lane highway which runs along its top the structure is only forty-five feet thick.

The task facing the builders was monumental.

To bring in the necessary equipment and materials a special railroad was built to connect with the main line at Las Vegas. To provide electricity for construction, a high power transmission line was run more than 200 miles across the desert from San Bernardino. A town came ready made off the drawing boards to house thousands of workers who came from all over the country. In contrast to earlier boom towns, this settlement did not die when the construction job was finished; it remains as a government-owned community today.

That perplexing old problem of the desert, transportation, rose to plague the dam builders, just as it had the silver and borax miners and the men who carried the mail. Pipes too huge to haul in by train or highway were called for. The solution was both simple and expensive: a factory to make them was built at the edge of the canyon.

The river had to be dried up at the place where the dam was to rise. But there was no place to divert the water except through the solid stone of the canyon walls. Engineers decided to drill four diversion tunnels through the cliffs, two on each side of the river, in such a way that they later could be used as an integral part of the dam's electricity generating system.

Months of dynamiting and blasting created tunnels, which were lined with a three-foot thickness of concrete. Thousands of tons of rock and earth made temporary dams just above and below the outlets. When the water between was pumped out, the ancient bed of the Colorado lay bare and empty for the first time in several thousand years.

Daredevil high scalers took over to cut niches in the rock to anchor the concrete structures. No machine could do this perilous job. Dangling by ropes hundreds of feet above the river bottom, courageous men hammered holes for explosive charges into the stone with mallets and long chisels. In summer the desert heat approached 130 degrees, and in winter sand-laden winds chilled their hands into numbness. Seven high scalers perished before the task was done.

At last all was ready to build the dam itself. More than

two years had been spent in preparatory construction before the first bucket of concrete was lifted and poured. The date was June 6, 1933. Nature cannot be conquered in a hurry.

By the time the last decorative post atop the dam was built two years later, the tremendous total of 8,500,000 tons of concrete had been mixed, hauled to the site and poured. The concrete used at Hoover Dam would make a sidewalk five feet wide the whole length of the earth from the North Pole to the South Pole!

Here the designers ran into another perplexing problem. "How can we get the cement to cool fast enough?" they asked. Mathematicians calculated that if the dam were allowed to cool without artificial aid, more than 150 years would elapse until it was chilled to the same temperature as the stone cliffs to which it was attached.

The builders hit upon the idea of an ice water cooling system. Concrete was poured in vertical columns, in layers five feet deep. A network of one-inch pipe at five-foot intervals crisscrossed inside the concrete as the dam rose, layer by layer. Through these pipes ice water was pumped at temperatures a few degrees above freezing, cooling the structure at a rapid and controlled pace. Instead of jagged cracks, only small gaps appeared between the vertical columns, and these were filled with cement.

The dam was built inward from each canyon wall toward the center. A gap eight feet wide was left in the middle. Through this the workmen were able to manipulate the cooling pipes. As the structure rose, cement was pumped into the pipes and they were sealed into the dam forever. By this ingenious method the entire dam was cooled in twenty months instead of 150 years.

Work went on day and night. Strings of searchlights were installed, many of them suspended by cables across the gorge, and after dark the dam took on the appearance of a giant fairyland in the middle of the desert.

Operation of the giant power plant, officially named Hoover Dam and dedicated by President Franklin D. Roosevelt in September, 1935, began in the fall of that year. At last the desert's mighty river was truly conquered.

The immensity of the man-made structure necessary to tame this area of the desert region is difficult to visualize. But enough water passes through the water wheels *every second* to fill a million quart bottles.

Backed up behind the dam is the world's largest artificial lake. Extending 115 miles upstream and with a maximum depth of 589 feet, Lake Mead holds enough water to cover the entire state of Connecticut with a layer ten feet deep. Seventy miles downstream is a secondary structure, the Davis Dam. Still further south is Parker Dam, and the All-American Canal and branch canals are part of the elaborate river control system that forms a scientific and safe means of irrigation for the desert farmlands.

The residents of the Imperial Valley have a permanent reminder of their flood disaster. The Salton Sea, formed when the rampaging Colorado poured into the below-sea-level saucer, still exists, kept at a constant level by water from the irrigation system. Boating and fishing enthusiasts have a lake thirty-five miles long in the middle of the desert for their vacation fun.

Lieutenant Ives would be unable to pilot his *Explorer* up the Colorado River now because of all the dams. But Americans who set out in their automobiles on the modern version of exploring, known as sightseeing, have two of the country's most spectacular sights awaiting them here in the heart of the desert. At the Grand Canyon, 200 miles upstream from Hoover Dam, they will see what nature has created through erosion and the cutting force of the Colorado River.

From there a drive of only a few hours brings them to man's impressive achievement in his fight to put the American wastelands to use.

By harnessing its turbulent river, men have taken a long step toward making the desert serve them.

12 The Desert Goes to Work

The attitude of Americans toward their gigantic desert has changed. Their dread of its perils and rigors has turned into fascinated interest and appreciation of its wonders. The tall arms of the saguero cactus beckon from hundreds of tourist advertisements.

"Let's go to the desert" has become an alluring invitation. It is the password for fun and leisurely living, jobs, bountiful farm lands, mineral wealth and enormous military bases.

The desert has gone to work. Having mastered many of its secrets, men are using it to produce food and wealth. They have found that vital commodity, oil, beneath its sands in some regions. They are using its sprawling spaces as a place to create this country's most advanced defense techniques and to develop new sources of power. In secret installations far from the cities Americans are learning the skills which may one day permit them to soar into space.

Wherever men can bring water, the desert soil blooms and air-conditioned cities grow. Where they cannot, the land is as stark and arid as it appeared to the few hungry Indian bands who roamed in search of food two thousand years ago.

One-sixth of the land in the continental United States is desert, and nature has put severe limits on what men can do with the desert. But the things they have accomplished there are remarkable, and even more spectacular achievements lie ahead.

The calendar showed July, 1945. Far away in the moist islands of the Pacific Ocean huge American armies and naval forces were readied for the climax of World War II, the invasion of Japan. But something was happening on the hot desert sands of southern New Mexico, too.

Extreme security regulations kept the words "atomic bomb" from the world, and only a few men knew the stupendous secret of what was to be attempted. Only after an atomic bomb had been dropped on Hiroshima, bringing about Japan's surrender without an invasion, did people learn of that first explosion at the secret test site on the American desert.

Midsummer heat had fallen upon the remote area of arid land as a small force of sweltering soldiers and scientists near Alamogordo made ready for the test.

The bomb parts were assembled at a ranch house. Two miles away a steel tower 110 feet tall was constructed. It stood in a wide sweeping desert valley, with the sandy soil broken only by patches of lava from ancient volcanoes. The desert was the only suitable place for experimenting with such an explosive force.

On the crucial day the bomb was placed atop the tower, and observers watched from a heavily protected shelter. The countdown was given. At zero, the desert was illuminated with a searing light that had the intensity of the mid-day sun. In the words of one observer, "It was golden, purple, violet, grey, blue . . . unprecedented, magnificent, beautiful, stupendous and terrifying."

The atomic age had opened.

From this start, the desert has become a mammoth workshop for military and scientific activities.

Gigantic areas, almost empty of inhabitants, provide excellent conditions for gunnery practice and weapons experiments. Secrecy is easily maintained, too. Behind signs which state, "KEEP OUT. Military reservation," guided missiles are being fired high in the desert sky.

At the Air Force Missile Development Center at Alamogordo there is a track seven miles long where the secrets of space flight are investigated, right on the ground. Test missiles are harnessed to a sled which hurtles along the track at four times the speed of sound. With its odd braking system of wooden barriers and water pools stored between the rails, scientists can recover the missile and study the efficiency of its firing apparatus.

Edwards Air Force base—spreading over 300,000 acres in the Mojave desert—is the home of the hottest airplanes the United States possesses. Every day the sky is abuzz with an assortment of fighters, bombers, tankers, helicopters. Every type of aircraft accepted for use by the Air Force must be put through rigorous trials by the test pilots at Edwards. Experimental and research planes also are flown here, and on the ridge across the dry lake bed stands the highly restricted rocket engine test laboratory.

Yucca Flat is a barren, virtually uninhabited plain in southwestern Nevada. For hundreds of years it lay dry and useless, crossed occasionally by a wandering Indian or prospector. Then the United States government developed the atomic bomb. It needed a place for further experimental explosions, where atomic blasts could be set off safely under proper wind condition and little danger. Only the desert could provide such a place. Dozens of nuclear devices have been exploded on the Yucca Flat proving ground without serious radiation effects.

Several hundred persons assembled on this plain in the moonlight one spring night. The visitors knew it was empty desert, yet, oddly, there rose before them a small town. The town even had a name, Survival City.

For a few hours this dateline appeared on headlined

news dispatches around the world. Then it disappeared, a ghost town of the nuclear age. This was a ghost town unlike the mining settlements of the desert, however, because it had never been inhabited by anything but wax manikins dressed to look like people.

Survival City had all the physical elements of a small modern community. The main street was named Doomsday Drive. There were houses of brick, wood and cement, several industrial buildings, electricity, a 250-watt radio transmitter, television sets, natural gas and a dial telephone system. Automobiles were parked outside the houses. A million dollars went into the building and equipping of Survival City. The purpose of this test was to see how well typical American homes and furnishings could stand up against an atomic explosion. The knowledge gained would be used by the Civil Defense organization.

As the observers huddled within the safety of heavily armored military tanks, the little community lay quiet, like any sleeping town. Three-quarters of a mile beyond Doomsday Drive, on a steel tower rising 500 feet above the desert, rested a nuclear device approximately twice as powerful as the first atomic bomb dropped on Japan.

The countdown reached zero, and a glaring light of overwhelming intensity illuminated the desert as the equivalent of 70,000,000 pounds of TNT exploded.

Hours later, after tests showed that the radiation had diminished, observers entered Survival City to see how it had fared. Although two houses of brick and wood had been smashed flat, and two industrial buildings were

wrecked, the structures of concrete blocks and cement remained standing. But windows were broken everywhere. Deadly slivers of glass had been hurled across the rooms like lances. Refrigerators and cars buckled or "exploded." Under the debris in the rooms lay the wax manikins.

After close study the expert verdict was, "It is doubtful if many occupants of Survival City would have escaped critical injury or death unless they had taken proper shelter. Had they done so, many might have escaped."

The desert at work means other things, too; the most fascinating of these is farming. Watching what can be grown from the dry and apparently useless ground when water is poured upon it is a never-ending wonder.

Irrigation is the tool which makes desert farming possible. This is not a new idea, for it has been used in various parts of the world for hundreds of years. Modern engineers have made irrigation a fine science, but in Arizona some of the water ditches near Phoenix follow closely those gouged in the desert with primitive tools hundreds of years ago by the long-vanished Hohokem people.

At the edge of an irrigated field the green ends suddenly; a single step carries a man from ripening crops to the parched nakedness of the desert. From the air these irrigated fields look like a patchwork of precisely-cut green squares laid upon an ancient, washed-out sheet of sand.

The water for irrigated fields comes from two sources, wells dug deep into the earth and canals which carry the life-giving fluid from the few dammed-up streams of the desert. Some wells go down 1,500 feet—more than the height of the Empire State building—and the water is pumped to the surface at high speed, as much as 500 gallons a minute. The throb of the pump hour after hour through the night is a familiar sound in irrigated farmlands. Farming by such methods is very expensive, but the soil yields two or more crops a year.

The pioneer American experiment in making the desert green was carried out a hundred years ago by the Mormons. This band of religious pioneers came westward in 1847 and settled on the desert near the Great Salt Lake. Bit by bit they developed an irrigation system which made their lands a showplace of the desert.

166

The reclaimed land of the Imperial Valley has become one of the most bountiful farm regions in the world, providing a wealth of melons, corn, cotton, citrus fruit, carrots and other vegetables. A heat-seared portion of Arizona desert, across which the pioneers of the southern trail once struggled, has been turned into a mammoth cotton field and vegetable garden by irrigation.

Desert farmers fight an endless battle against insects which thrive in the dry warmth. Clouds of poisonous insecticides are sprayed by crop-dusting planes. Pilots of these old-fashioned biplanes put on a purposeful display of acrobatics in order to reach every corner of the fields.

Farmers of the Imperial Valley, faced with an invasion of their alfalfa fields by aphids, contrived a strange but victorious combination to halt the pestilence—wasps and a giant vacuum cleaner. Colonies of wasps, which eat aphids, are planted in an infested field. When they have devoured the injurious pests, an oversize vacuum cleaner is driven around the field on a truck. It sucks up the masses of wasps, which are then released in another threatened alfalfa field. The battle to wrest crops from the desert requires patience, vigor and ingenuity.

With irrigation performing wonders, and such a vast amount of desert lying idle, can we count upon reclaiming more and more land to feed our country's swiftly-increasing population?

Unfortunately, this possibility is limited. In some regions which depend upon deep wells, farmers already are overdrawing their water "bank account," and the underground water level is falling. The desert still is resisting man's ingenious efforts to subdue it.

However, a new possibility is arising, and perhaps some day it will be applied to dry-land farming. Engineers have long talked about taking the salt out of sea water and making the purified liquid available for human use. They know how to do this in small quantities, but the process is extremely expensive. Now they are working on methods to desalt sea water with atomic power. The time may come when the ocean is piped to the desert, and together they will produce food for the tables of the world.

The most exotic crop grown on the desert is dates. Although the graceful arms of the date palm are a favorite symbol of artists depicting the desert, few of them are to be found anywhere in the American desert lands outside the Coachella Valley of Southern California, only a few miles long. But their cultivation is another fascinating desert story.

Growing as high as a six-story building and spreading its fan-like fronds majestically, the date palm must be nursed like an infant if it is to produce fruit. While its head soaks up the desert sunshine, its feet must stand deep in cool water. The combination of continuous hot, dry air and an abundance of irrigation water makes the Coachella Valley exactly right for production of the luscious, dainty sweetmeat.

A half century ago 129 young date palms were brought

over from North Africa for the first commercial date garden in America. There are male and female palms and the transfer of male pollen to the fruit-bearing female must be done by humans if they are to produce an abundant crop. At such great heights, date palm gardeners need very high ladders. The fruit is often gathered from a high metal scaffolding on wheels.

Rain, so welcome during the growing season of other crops, may be a calamity to the date grower. Moisture causes infection in the fruit, and a water-resistant bag is tied around each cluster. At a glance, each bagged tree looks as though it is bearing a cluster of bells.

As in the days of the prospectors and overnight riches in gold and silver, the desert is still a treasure house of mineral wealth. From deep in the arid earth comes the mineral that makes the wonders of the atomic age possible—uranium.

A generation ago miners kicked uranium ore aside as waste, much as the pioneers ignored borax. It had no value because nobody had a use for it. Now it is among the most wanted minerals on earth.

Once more Uncle Sam has turned to his desert storehouse for needed supplies. Uranium has been found in remote corners of the parched wastelands of the West, especially in areas adjacent to the Four Corners. Sparsely populated and rarely visited, this lonely patch of desert lies northeast of the Grand Canyon in the land of the Navajos. A cement marker two feet high stands as a sen-

169

tinel on the arid plain. When a person walks around the monument he has, within thirty seconds, been in four states—Arizona, New Mexico, Utah and Colorado. This is an artificial boundary; no natural terrain features dictate the location of the marker.

The discovery of uranium and oil in this far-off corner of the country has brought a bustle of activity. At first lone prospectors roamed the region with Geiger counters. Now, uranium production on the desert has been taken over by large companies which employ thousands of men.

Oil, uranium and borax are the glamor products of today's desert mines. A bounty of other minerals, essential to American industry, also come from the heat-baked desert. These mines range from the mammoth open copper pits of Arizona to small isolated diggings at the end of single dirt tracks winding back into the dusty hills. Among their products are phosphorus, mica, barite, cinnabar, manganese, salts and bentonite, a pure clay that swells in water, useful in oil fields and foundries.

The desert is a lonely place, where a man in search of solitude can walk for days without seeing another human. And yet, in contrast, it has become the site of bustling, neon-lighted cities with tens of thousands of permanent inhabitants who work in factories and stores.

Las Vegas, Nevada, once was a water hole on the old Spanish trail from Salt Lake to the pueblo of Los Angeles. Today it is a fabulous resort city in the middle of the desert. Magnificent hotels, one of them a skyscraper, provide world-renowned entertainers and luxurious accommodations.

On weekends the 275-mile highway across the eroded plains and dry lake beds from Las Vegas to Los Angeles is bumper-to-bumper with automobiles. Their headlights make an almost unbroken streak of light for dozens of miles. Yet the inquisitive motorist who, obeying an impulse, turns off this crowded highway at one of the side trails is so isolated on the primitive desert within ten minutes that he may feel as though he has entered a silent world all his own.

What the desert lacks in water it makes up with an overflowing abundance of nature's other life-giving resource, sunshine. Holiday-makers at poolsides and astride dude ranch horses toast themselves a fashionable brown. The sun's rays, beaming down day after day without a cloud to hide them, ripen desert farm crops quickly. They warm the bones of easy-going dwellers. For most desert folk, the all-embracing sunshine is a boon, although they sometimes would like to turn it off for a few hours in midsummer. For the occasional wanderer who, even today, gets lost in the vastness it can be a scourge.

Now scientists are putting the sunshine of the desert to work in a new and intriguing way, through the capture of solar energy. The possibilities of sun power excite the imagination. The small amount of research done thus far has shown that the rays of the sun, when captured and

171

stored up, can heat a house and also cool it, run clocks, radios and electric razors and keep the waters of the family swimming pool pleasantly warm the year around.

A solar house has been built near Phoenix, where the sun does the heating and cooling work the entire year. It looks much like an ordinary one-story home of the informal western style, except for sixty-eight louvers, adjustable slanting pieces of aluminum and blackened copper, which are lined up above the patios. These resemble the wings of an airplane. Each louver contains tubes through which water is pumped.

The sun's energy is trapped by the louvers, converted into heat by the blackened copper and passed into the circulating water at a temperature of 140 degrees. This hot water is pumped into an underground storage tank. When heat is needed in the house, circulating air is warmed by the hot water. For cooling, the heat pump valve is turned to supply a cold refrigerant which cools the air entering the house; the big louvers are turned down to provide shade.

At Palm Springs, California, an outdoor clock is powered by the sun's rays. Silicon cells convert the light energy into usable electricity, which is stored in a battery; thus there is power to run the clock's machinery at night and on cloudy days.

Looking into the future, the day may come when the world's underground supply of gas, oil and coal is exhausted. Fortunately the energy of the sun is endless and waiting to work for men, once they have learned how to use it efficiently. And nowhere is it so readily available as on the sweeping expanse of the desert.

This is our challenging desert: the land of little rain where men have found satisfaction and an elusive beauty in their fight to conquer inhospitable nature.

For thousands of years primitive men scratched out a skimpy existence in the arid lands that form a barrier across the western part of the United States. Their ambition was merely to survive the desert's hardships; through the centuries they gradually found the scattered havens where this could be done. With few exceptions they used the resources easily at hand, without trying to explore the desert's hidden wealth.

The Spaniards came, bringing the white man's domestic animals, metal tools and firearms, and a new way of life. But these daring soldiers and determined priests were at the fringe of an empire whose center was thousands of miles away, on the other side of the Atlantic Ocean. There were too few of them to impose their will on the desert itself, although they did so with the Indians they found living there. Even at its highest point, the Spanish period on the southwestern desert was only a colonial occupation. Spanish influence never penetrated to the northern desert area.

A century ago, or a little more, the first venturesome Americans pushed westward into the desert and found it almost empty. This was the unwanted part of America, forbidding and grim, a land not easily comprehended by

173

those who had come from regions where the ground was green.

At first they could see only hardship and misery. The drab gray land was a dreaded, uncharted place to be crossed as quickly as possible. Men died by the hundreds, and their property was strewn along the desert trails as the emigration pushed westward. The discovery of gold in California gave this trek a tremendous impetus.

Gradually some of the emigrants stopped off to try their luck at desert living, and settlements began. They devised ways to cope with the extreme heat that smothers the desert five months of the year—tricks like soaking their sheets in water when they went to bed, in the hope that they could fall asleep before the cool dampness evaporated. They used their mechanical skills to make life easier and to probe beneath the desert's surface. At some places they found water, in others a mass of minerals.

As men learned to accept the desert's terms, they found it a place of unique charm. Boundless space and a towering blue sky engulfed them; the bustle of huge cities was far away and there seemed little need to hurry.

The desert today is partially tamed. Hundreds of bungalows on five-acre homesteads are sprinkled through some of its dry basins like chopped nuts scattered on a cake frosting. Air conditioning keeps homes and offices comfortable even when the thermometer outside reads 120 degrees, as it often does in some areas during midsummer. Major highways stretch the length and breadth of the dry one-sixth of our country.

Yet, although it has been bent to man's uses, the desert is not yet fully conquered. Sandstorms billowing unchecked across the treeless plains strip the paint from automobiles and sometimes force the closing of highways. Thunderstorms erode the barren hills and the beating sun restricts human activities.

This is a land of many moods, mellow warmth, smothering heat and, at times, bone-chilling cold, harsh storms or silent crimson sunsets. Most of all it is a land of unlimited space—a land where courageous men have fought and struggled to make their mark, but have only dented the vastness. The challenge remains, fascinating and compelling, the last frontier within the continental United States.

The Author

Residing in Indio, California, Phil Ault knows the desert region well, and his extensive experience as a newspaperman lends a dramatic story-telling quality to his skillful handling of the desert's exciting story.

A former war correspondent and manager of the United Press London Bureau, Mr. Ault served as assistant managing editor of the Los Angeles *Mirror-News* from 1948 to 1957 and is now Executive Editor of the Associated Desert Newspapers of California. Co-author of SPRINGBOARD TO BERLIN and REPORTING THE NEWS, this is his first book for young people.

The Artist

Leonard Everett Fisher, whose black and white line drawings vividly portray the mood of the desert and the amazing events that took place there, is the winner of a Pulitzer Art Prize and awards by the American Institute of Graphic Arts. His outstanding illustrations have appeared in numerous books for young readers.